LEGENDS OF THE MENDI VALLEY

Footprints of the Coming of the Gospel

LEGENDS OF THE MENDI VALLEY

Footprints of the Coming of the Gospel

by

Stella Sondpi

Legends of the Mendi Valley
by Stella Sondpi

Text and pictures copyright © Stella Sondpi 2025
All rights reserved

In accordance with copyright laws, this book or parts thereof may not be reproduced in any form, stored in an retrieval system, or transmitted in any form by any means - electronic, mechanical, photocopy, recording, or otherwise - without prior written permission of the publisher or author.

No AI Training: Without in any way limiting the author's exclusive rights under copyright, any use of this publication to "train" generative artificial intelligence (AI) technologies to generate text is expressly prohibited. The author reserves all rights to license uses of this work for generative AI training and development of machine learning language models.

Published by Nenge Books, Australia, June 2025
ABN 26809396184
nengebooks1@gmail.com
www.nengebooks.com

Scripture quotations marked [GNT] are taken from Good News Translation® (Today's English Version, Second Edition) © 1992 American Bible Society. All rights reserved.
Bible text from the Good News Translation (GNT) is not to be reproduced in copies or otherwise by any means except as permitted in writing by American Bible Society, 101 North Independence Mall East, FL 8, Philadelphia, PA 19106 -2155 USA (www.americanbible.org).

Scripture quotations marked (NLT) are taken from the Holy Bible, New Living Translation, copyright ©1996, 2004, 2015 by Tyndale House Foundation. Used by permission of Tyndale House Publishers, Carol Stream, Illinois 60188. All rights reserved.

Scripture quotations marked [NIV] are taken from The Holy Bible, New International Version® NIV® Copyright © 1973, 1978, 1984, 2011 by Biblica, Inc. Used with permission. All rights reserved worldwide.

Scripture quotations marked [NASB] are taken from the (NASB®) New American Standard Bible®, Copyright © 1960, 1971, 1977, 1995 by The Lockman Foundation. Used by permission. All rights reserved. lockman.org

Scripture quotations marked [KJV] are from The Authorized (King James) Version. Rights in the Authorized Version in the United Kingdom are vested in the Crown. Reproduced by permission of the Crown's patentee, Cambridge University Press

Scripture quotations marked [ESV] are from the ESV® Bible (The Holy Bible, English Standard Version®), © 2001 by Crossway, a publishing ministry of Good News Publishers. ESV Text Edition: 2025. The ESV text may not be quoted in any publication made available to the public by a Creative Commons license. The ESV may not be translated in whole or in part into any other language. Used by permission. All rights reserved."

ISBN 978-0-6459597-8-9

Dedication

This book is dedicated to the People of Mendi Valley in the Southern Highlands Province of Papua New Guinea.

We have been through a lot together as Southern Highlanders. Negativity poured in from the rest of the country and maybe the world as Political issues and other National Disasters like the 7.5 magnitude Earthquake hit us.

But be blessed to know that God had already existed in our cultures and He will continue to be with us till the end. God bless Southern Highlands.

From one human being he created all races of people and made them live throughout the whole earth. He himself fixed beforehand the exact times and the limit of the places where they would live. He did this so that they would look for him, and perhaps find him as they felt around for Him. Yet God is actually not far from any one of us;
Acts 17:26-27 [GNT]

Contents

FOREWORD ix
INTRODUCTION 1
PART A 3
LEGENDS OF THE CHILDREN OF MENDI VALLEY
Legend One   TAR MAN PAPLIN 5
Legend Two   THE TWELVE BROTHERS 14
Legend Three   POREAH HINN KOLUM 22
Legend Four   THE CHEATING CUSCUS 27
Legend Five   THE TALKING TARO 33
Legend Six   THE EVIL GRANDMOTHER 37
Legend Seven   THE TWO BROTHERS 45
Legend Eight   THE SECRET GROOM 53
Legend Nine   WAR WITH THE GIANTS 62
Legend Ten   THE CALLING OF THE RISING SMOKE 69
PART B 77
EVIDENCE OF YAWEH'S FOOTPRINT IN THE TEN LEGENDS
Footprint One   TAR MAN PAPLIN & IP TEKES PIU 81
Footprint Two   THE TWELVE BROTHERS 89
Footprint Three PORFAH HINN & KOLUM 94
Footprint Four   THE CHEATING CUSCUS 99
Footprint Five   THE TALKING TARO 103
Footprint Six   THE EVIL GRANDMOTHER 110
Footprint Seven THE TWO BROTHERS 117
Footprint Eight THE SECRET GROOM 126
Footprint Nine   WAR WITH THE GIANTS 133
Footprint Ten   THE CALLING OF THE RISING SMOKE 137

FOREWORD

Culture has at times been portrayed as bad, even evil, something that people need to move on from to demonstrate a true faith in God. So it is against that negative paradigm that Stella Sondpi seeks to offer a contradictory view - that God has been present in tribal cultures well before their 'discovery' by missionaries and the rest of the world. These oral cultures have a rich heritage of stories and legends passed down faithfully through the generations. The key is in understanding the deeper meaning and significance of these narratives, like an overlay of meaning beyond the actual storyline.

Building on her first book, POMBREOL, stories of pre-first contact life in the Mendi valley of Papua New Guinea told her by her grandfather, Stella digs into ten legends in her tribe. The concept of Biblically-based spiritual truths embedded in culture was expounded by former missionary in Irian Jaya, Don Richardson, in his book, *"Eternity in Their Hearts"*. He proposed that God has never left people groups devoid of witness and in fact, within various customs and tribal narratives are redemptive keys which are fulfilled when the full gospel message of redemption in Christ is received. Take, for example, the practice of blood sacrifice so common in Melanesia, or the acknowledgement of a Creator.

It is important that those engaged in missionary and gospel outreach, whether locally or internationally, recognise that God has already been at work in cultures, and they don't step into a spiritual vacuum. When the deeper significance of cultural context is understood, response to the gospel is always much greater, as Stella herself testifies within her own tribal group.

I am thankful for the opportunity to publish this work, which adds understanding to the task of cross-cultural gospel outreach and the recognition that we seek to appreciate where God has already been at work in a culture, preparing them for the coming of the message of Christ.

Michael Jelliffe
Nenge Books

INTRODUCTION

"For ever since the world was created, people have seen the earth and sky. Through everything God made, they can clearly see His invisible qualities - His eternal power and divine nature. So they have no excuse for not knowing God".
Romans 1:20 [NLT]

God truly set eternity in the hearts of the men and women of the world, and the people of the Mendi valley were not an exception. Their way of living, culture, traditions and nature itself continued to reflect God Yahweh and His existence, even before the arrival of the Gospel of Christ through missionaries.

In this book, the existence of God's Word in customs, cultures and nature are discussed. The very culture and surroundings of the Mendi valley acted as God's missionaries and testified to His existence.

Even if the missionaries were quiet, the stones themselves would start shouting, as stated in Luke 19:40. If the stones refused, then the animals, or the birds in the sky, or the fish in the rivers, would start teaching about the hand of God, as Job 12:7-10 proclaims.

However, those cultures, traditions and nature could not bring the people of the Mendi valley into direct contact with

God, for they reveal the power of God without revealing His personhood. These people needed more than the testimony of nature to understand who God is, and what He requires of us.

Creation gives only a partial perception of God. So the children of the Mendi valley, in their limitations as human beings as well as their sinful nature, were not competent to understand any more about God until the missionaries came in with the gospel of truth and light, which enlightened their dark minds. The people then accepted the gospel quickly as the culture and customs had traces of God's Word, which paved the way for the people.

This book is divided into two parts. Part One is a collection of ten famous legends from the valley. Part Two explains the Word of God hidden in the legends in Part One, God's footprints in the culture, leading to the coming of the Gospel.

Nuggets of truth hidden in the legends and customs are exposed and the Word of God is provided as a proof to declare that God had planted His word of Truth among the cultures and customs of the people of this valley, even before the Gospel came in.

Stella Sondpi
Mendi, SHP, PNG
November 2024

PART A

LEGENDS OF THE CHILDREN OF MENDI VALLEY

There are many indigenous languages in the world that have no written form. Cultures with unwritten languages are rich in oral tradition, stories, songs and poetry. Through them, stories reinforcing their cultures are passed from one generation to another, maintaining consistency and reliability through the times. Research by scientists is finding more evidence of events that happened thousands of years ago which have been documented and carefully preserved in indigenous story telling.

Legends of the Mendi Valley

Legend One

TAR MAN PAPLIN

Once upon a time, in the beautiful Mendi valley, lived the prettiest young girl, called 'Tar Man Paplin'.

She lived alone in the forest with her parents. The only thing she could ever do was to dance. Each day from sunrise to sunset, she would sway gracefully to the melody of her own kundu drum. She enjoyed herself so much that she was never bothered by the fact that there was no audience to appreciate her performances.

She could only stop for a while during lunch hour, and then rest when the sun had set, and darkness has arrived. Pumpkin cooked in hot ashes was her only food and this was cooked by her parents. Because she was an only child, her parents took care of her like a princess.

The forest she lived in was surrounded by tall mountains and rugged rocks, forming a strong barrier which made it impossible for anybody from the outside world to enter her side of the land.

Beyond the rugged mountains lay a whole valley full of people unknown to Tar Man Paplin and her parents. This group of people would hear the beat of the kundu drum from beyond the impenetrable blue mountains. They tried all kinds of ways to enter the valley but for a long time no one was ever successful.

As each day passed, the melody produced by the beating of her kundu drum became more attractive and irresistible. This beat had a special ring to it, appealing to all the young men in the land. So they tried all kinds of ways and techniques to climb over the mountain, but no one was ever successful.

Again and again they would try climbing, but could never find a way to climb up the rock right to the top. The surrounding rocks, tall mountains and terrain were impossible for any human to climb. Every man in the valley who tried gave up after numerous attempts.

But there was one particular young man called Ip Tekes Piu who never gave up. The melody seemed to have a special meaning for him and him only. His thoughts would wander away and fly to that land on the other side of the mountains. Every passing day he would dream away. His heart would never know any rest as long as that kundu drum beat existed. There was something about that rhythm that had a special connection to his own heartbeat. Sometimes he was sure he could hear the melody whispering his name and calling him to the forest.

The desire to see the owner of this kundu beat was such that no other experience in the world could satisfy him. He felt he was meant for that world on the other side of the mountain. He longed for it so deeply that he was not able to rest until he could find his rest and peace in that land beyond. He felt he was set apart for that land and that he had to pay his price by climbing the steep rock. But how to climb that rock, he had no idea at all.

One such restless night, he had fallen asleep in the men's house on the hard earth. He fell into a deep sleep when a rat came by and spread out his long ears, forming a sleeping mat on the ground. The rat then rolled Ip Tekes Piu over onto the mat, rolled him up and carried him towards the rugged mountains.

At the bottom of the mountain, the rat told him to look carefully at the bare rocks before him. As Ip Tekes Piu examined the rocks carefully, the rat asked if he could see something and, of course, there was a fine bush vine hidden among the rocks.

As he turned around to say he could see a bush vine on the rock, he saw that the rat had disappeared. He opened his eyes and to his great surprise, he found himself at the foot of the mountain. As he slowly turned around again, the rope was right there actually on the spot he had seen in his dream. He couldn't believe what was happening.

He quickly grabbed the vine and tried to pull it down but it would not easily dislodge. Knowing that he would be safe, and looking around to make sure nobody was around, he quickly clung to the rope and slowly climbed up it.

As he climbed up with sweat pouring down his forehead, even in the cool morning air, he did not have the guts to look down again for fear had gripped his very heart. Strong cold winds from the valley below were blowing up angrily at him, as if he was trespassing. He could feel all the hairs in his body rising and goose bumps growing all over his body. Any wrong turn, move or twist and he would fall to his death.

He closed his eyes to lock out such frightening thoughts and with sheer determination pulled himself up to the very top of the mountain. Keeping his eyes closed, he lay there for a while till he was no longer dizzy, then opened his eyes.

Sitting up quickly, he looked below to where he had come from and his heart missed a beat. The valley was far below him. As he turned to face the opposite direction, he was amazed at the way Mother Nature was presenting to him the pure beauty of the surrounding, undisturbed mountains.

He observed that the mountain top that he was sitting on directly faced another mountain and the two mountains had created a valley between them. This valley was sitting gracefully right before his eyes, displaying all its hidden glory. He was so deeply immersed in this wonder of nature. There was something in the surroundings that uplifted him. He felt as if nature was communicating with him directly by the breeze that passed by him, rustling through the trees, undergrowth and flowers. The birds that were singing cheerfully from nearby trees in the thick forest sounded strange to his ears. The environment was so undisturbed that for a moment he forgot the reason for this trip. The sheer beauty of the surrounding area took his breath away. He felt as if this was totally another world and he was indeed made for this brand-new world. There definitely were no traces of humans in the area, making him feel like an alien.

To that new world he will go but, after seeking the way for a very long time, he wondered how he got himself to the top to enjoy all this beauty. His path was fixed by a rat from his dream and now he was right on top of the world. Strange things were happening indeed, but for now, it was a dream come true for him and so he must live that dream to reality now.

As his eyes took in every part of the beauty displayed before him, he could feel Mother Nature seducing him, tranquilising him to sleep. As he struggled against drooping eyelids from the strong anaesthesia in the air, he sat down where he stood and gave way to the heavy sleep that was closing in on him.

Before he fell into a deep sleep, he heard a strange sound rising from the deep valley up to the mountain top. The sound was so sweet yet familiar. He momentarily forgot his drooping eyelids and sat up quickly. As he sat still to listen to the sound properly, he knew what it was. It was the gentle beating of the kundu drum.

But the melody that rose was different from what he had been hearing on the other side of the mountain. This time it was a melody that was rising beautifully across the whole sleeping valley, gracefully in all its majesty. In the still air, the beating of the kundu drum sounded almost like his own heartbeat as it thumped strongly against his chest. The melody was rising from deep within the valley and he must get to its very source.

He looked around in desperation to find a way to go to the source of this melody but could not find a track. Then he found the other end of the same vine that he had climbed up and slowly climbed down into the unknown valley below.

At the foot of the mountain, as he walked towards the melody, he could feel the environment staring back at him as if to tell him that he was an intruder and that his presence was not welcomed. He quickened his steps and walked in fear and trepidation as he drew closer to the sound. Very tall trees dwarfed him as he walked by. Even the rivers and creeks seemed to be silently following him. They seemed to be communicating among themselves, making him feel even more like an intruder among them.

He walked on until he came to a clearing. As he stared into the face of the prettiest girl he had ever seen in all his life, his heart stopped beating for a second. He just stood there staring and staring at this beauty, dancing gracefully to the beat of her kundu, oblivious to his presence. Since there was no audience, he stood transfixed, totally entranced by her beauty and the gracefulness of her dance. Her beauty was breath taking.

After what seemed to be a long time, someone tapped his arm. He jumped up, only to find the gentle arm of a woman and a man who stood right behind him, their faces stern.

The man was the first one to talk. With an expressionless face, he asked Ip Tekes Piu from which direction he came, because there was absolutely no way in or out of this valley. In a very soft voice, Ip Tekes Piu explained himself. He also told them about the struggles of other young men who wanted to come to see the source of the melody produced by this beating of the kundu drum.

To his surprise, they both softened up and invited him to their home. He stayed with them for few full moons, constantly observing how the parents treated their daughter. He also started helping in preparing her lunch and other things, such as body decorations for her dance.

One day he told them he wanted to go back to his part of the land and asked if they could release their daughter to go with him. After discussing it for a long time, the parents agreed to let her go with him, on the grounds that he take care of her in the same way as they do. He readily agreed to that. That afternoon he was so happy that he was taking the beautiful girl home.

At the sound of the first morning bird, he took her home. This time even the most difficult road was made easy, as love was in the air. He led her where the road was easy and carried her on the difficult pathway until they reached his home.

Back in his village the next day, there was excitement in the air like never before. The most wanted beauty was being brought home. The road was made as smooth as possible and messages were passed around to fill every rough pathway lest her foot was hurt.

The only possessions the girl brought with her was her kundu drum and her dressing gear. Ip Tekes Piu announced to the people that, as of the next morning, Tar Man Paplin would start performing her dances and so people were welcomed to watch.

Word spread quickly that the source of that Kundu drum that had been attracting so many men was a beautiful woman, brought home by Ip Tekes Piu, who was performing every day in his village.

People came from far and near to watch her perform. She would dance so beautifully to the sound of her own Kundu drum. The people would stare at her as if it was their first time to see such a dance. She would stop only when the sun was high up in the sky for her lunch, which was only provided by Ip Tekes Piu and consisted of young pumpkin and soft greens. Every day she danced to the beat of her kundu drum with people coming to watch from far and near.

Until one fine day, when Ip Tekes Piu announced a trip to the East to see an uncle who was giving him a pig as a contribution towards the payment of Tar Man Paplin's bride price. He gave particular instructions to his mother, asking her to look after Tar Man Paplin's lunch. He told his mum that he will be gone for two days and begged her to be very diligent in taking care of Tar Man Paplin. The mother readily agreed and so he started his journey the next day. As he travelled, he heard the beating of the Kundu until he was far away and could hear it no more. He continued his journey with a heavy heart.

Back in the village, all went well that day. The next day, Tar Man Paplin danced as her admirers watched. As the sun rose to the middle of the sky, it was lunch time but no lunch was ready as it usually was. She rushed over to the fire place and tried to cook a pumpkin that was left there by her mother-in-law. Unfortunately, the hot ashes burned her soft fingers. Swinging her fingers in all directions because of the excruciating pain, she fled from the village and ran towards the sunset.

The next day, as Ip Tekes Piu was on his way back after his journey, he reached the top of the mountain and knew something was not right: he could not hear the kundu drum beat anymore. He walked further down and stopped to listen again for the sound of the Kundu drum, but all he could hear was his own heart beating so fast and strong within himself.

He started walking faster and faster until he arrived at the village nearby. An old woman in the village told him that the sound of the Kundu had been missing since midday yesterday. Today, she heard rumours in the area that Tar Man Paplin is also missing.

At that news, Ip Tekes Piu felt that his heart, which was beating so fast and strong within him, almost stopped. He tried to walk faster but his feet were too heavy. As he reached home, his house was cold. The fire had died and there was nobody around. As he looked around desperately for someone to feed him with news of the previous day's event, no one was around. The whole village seemed to be empty and a fear like never before gripped him.

He felt a sudden nausea which overtook him and he couldn't stop himself falling into a deep darkness. He didn't know how long he was lying there until he found himself being lifted by strong hands. His uncle and his son were talking to him. As he sat up and took in what they were saying, he sat up straighter.

Those surrounding him started telling him about Tar Man Paplin and how she had burnt her hands while making her lunch. She ran away into the sunset, they concluded. He got up quickly and followed her. Every village he passed through gave the same story. She had passed by yesterday without stopping or any word.

He followed until he came to the top of the mountain that shares the border between the Lai valley and the places where he had come from. As he reached the top of the mountain that divides the valley and his part of the land, he saw a lifeless figure lying on top of a stony hill that looked over the valley below. He stopped suddenly and breathed in the fresh air blowing up from the deep valley below. He kept his eyes below, avoiding gazing on the trek ahead of him as he was afraid of what he might find ahead. The sun was already setting over the mountains and sinking into the valley below. He knew darkness was not very far away and slowly turned towards the track. With a heavy heart, he walked towards the figure.

Upon reaching the spot, he saw it was Tar Man Paplin and quickly grabbed her. In desperation he tried to wake her up. She opened her eyes slowly and when she realised that it was Ip Tekes Piu, she told him to get a sharp stone and operate quickly on her. He refused to do that but to his dismay she died. Ip Tekes Piu was so shocked; he stood transfixed to the spot for a what seemed like a long time. He sat beside her and cried like never before. He wailed and cried for a very long time.

With no one around to share his sorrow, he took a grip on himself and decided to take her dying advice. He quickly grabbed a sharp stone and operated on her. To his delight, he found all kinds of rich ornaments and kina shells inside her. He got everything out and buried her on the site.

Once he reached home, he got his bow and arrow and shot his mum to death.

He has gotten rid of the evil and lived a happy man with all the riches given to him by Tar Man Paplin, his dead wife.

The End.

The gap formed by one mountain meeting the other mounmtain at Biwiri. Tar Man Paplin was found dead between the gaps on the spot where the child stands. She was on her way to the valley below.

Legend Two

THE TWELVE BROTHERS

Once upon a time, there lived a chief who had two wives. The first wife was from upstream while the second wife was from downstream on the mighty Lai River.

Their lives were simply the happiest as both wives had six sons each, totalling up to twelve. All twelve were strong and handsome boys and without wives. Their father would be heard talking about them with great pride in his voice.

One fine day, the eldest son told everyone he was going hunting in the high mountains surrounding their area. He took with him his bow and arrow and was heard by the rest of the family members whistling happily on the upward track that leads towards the tall mountain that towers beyond the hills. This mountain was known for housing thevbest cuscus.

As the day went by, the family waited in anticipation, as every hunting trip means decent meals when the hunter returns. At the expected time of arrival, the younger boys went up the hills to wait for their brother so they would happily help with the fresh bundles of food and ease his load as well. They waited and waited until dark. There was no sign of their elder brother. Sadly they walked home and told the waiting family that he didn't arrive.

In the days that followed, there was a sadness that overtook the home as their eldest son and brother had not returned from the hunting trip. After some time, the second born announced that he was going to look for his elder brother. He followed the same track but he too never returned from his trip.

This continued to happen until all eleven brothers went to the same hunting site by the same route and never returned home.

By this time, there was total sadness in the home of the chief. The two wives sat around the house and cried at every opportunity while the chief, whose sadness was too much to handle, refused to eat and sat around with ashes painted all over his body. The last son would roam around aimlessly in total boredom. All the laughter and games were a thing of the past now.

The last of the twelve sons announced he was following his brothers. The three old people refused to let him go until he carefully explained to them his plans for the journey.

After he was released to go on the dangerous journey, he took a different route to the mountains instead of the familiar and most often used track. As he reached the very top of the mountain, he laid down for a rest. After a good rest, he quickly sat up and looked down the valley below. The view of the whole valley was breathtaking. Very beautiful tall mountains surrounded the valley. He could even see a big river gracefully flowing down. This river was brown in colour and divided the valley into two separate valleys within the one main valley. As his eyes moved quickly around, taking in the sheer beauty of the land, his eyes brought him closer to the mountain he was sitting on.

To his great surprise, he saw a group of ladies working in a garden in the hot sun. He quickly ran down and hid himself behind a huge tree near the garden where the ladies were gardening. As he looked closely, he saw that all the ladies were beautiful and young. Among them was one who was breath-takingly beautiful. Her breasts were exceptionally young and her face was so pretty, he stared at her for a while. When she laughed from jokes cracked by the other girls, her teeth shined like the moon and all things stood still at the sound of her voice.

He quickly counted the women and realised there was ten of them and they were all sisters. He was deciding what to do next, until he heard them talking about taking a drinking break in the nearby creek. Running quickly over to the creek ahead of them, he turned himself into a mosquito. He flew above the water and waited patiently as each girl took their turn in drinking. Then came the beauty among them all. Thirstily, she opened her mouth to drink and right at that moment the mosquito got on the water and allowed himself to be swallowed.

As the days went by, the young girl who was the last born among them felt her body getting weaker and she felt sick, so she wasn't going to the garden with her sisters. As weeks passed by, she realised she was missing her periods.

To the uttermost surprise of her bigger sisters, she had became pregnant. Her sisters would ask whom she had laid down with but she honestly denied laying down with a man. They would ask again and again but she had no idea how she got pregnant, so they stopped tormenting her with questions and started taking care of her instead.

When the time came, she delivered a bouncing baby boy. All ten sisters poured all their love around him. At no time did they let him cry or go hungry or mistreat him. He was the precious cargo of the house. As he grew up, he grew up with the best of what the women could give him.

As soon as he started talking, he would ask after his father but nobody had any answers. The boy constantly brought up the subject of their origins and where his grandparents were but nobody wanted to talk and he was met by silent tares from all ten girls.

Over and over again he asked but the sisters would always change the subject. Soon he grew into a handsome and strong teenager. By this time he had control over everything and everyone in the house. Nobody dared to say anything against him for the fear of his deliberate questions regarding where their father was. He now understood that it was the greatest secret among the sisters. A secret they couldn't even tell him despite their great love for him.

One fine day, during the taro harvest season, it was the sisters' time to harvest their taro and repay people who had given them something during their harvest. On that day, people came from far and near. In the middle of the garden stood the biggest and healthiest of all the taros. The girls as one had decided that this one taro was for their only son. Every time they visited their gardens, the boy would go straight to his taro plant and admire it while his mother cleaned the garden, until the taros were ready to be harvested. As the harvest time was approaching, there was real excitement in the air. Relatives from far and near arrived for the great harvest.

At night, before the harvest time the next day, the young boy crept to the garden, harvested his own taro and threw it into the fast-flowing river that flowed close to the garden. Then he went back to his house and slept.

Knowing they had a long day ahead of them, his mother and her sisters went early to their garden for the great harvest. To their dismay, they saw that their son's taro was missing. They looked at each other in shocked disbelief and started crying.

As the sun rose, the boy came to the garden and was told of the event of the night. In great distress he quickly climbed up a big tree near the big river and followed one of its branches that ran across the river. He shouted to his panicking mother and her sisters that he would jump straight into the river to kill himself if his taro was not brought back to where it was.

The ladies all cut their fingers and ears but to no avail. They offered all the rest of the taro but he told them none of those taros matched the one belonging to him. In utter distress, the ladies called to him to come down quickly and they would take him to visit his grandfather the next day. To that he responded quickly and climbed down from the tree.

Early next morning, the mother and her son left the village to visit that unknown grandfather. As they journeyed upstream, they came to the foot of the mountain that separates their side of the valley from the grandfather's side of the valley, and the walking track end at the foot of the mountain.

As the young man looked around in desperation, his mother came forward with her walking stick called the 'Kam Yolip' and hit a piece of rock that was part of the bigger rock that had been the foundation of the mountain. As if by magic, the mountain suddenly divided into two, creating a pathway that seemed to be continuing on from the track that they had been walking on. The two of them walked through the mountain on the pathway that was provided. When they were on the other side, the mountain went back to its place. There was no way again to go back to their side.

As he looked around quickly, he saw that there was only one house. His mum quickly explained to him that her father was the only man who lived in this part of the land and the one house was her fathers. Because their father was unusual in his dealings, his existence was kept as top secret. She told him that because of his persistent questioning and the fear of losing him, because they love him so much he was brought to visit her father, so he had to be very obedient to him. This would win his favour.

His granddad was a very tall man with long wide beard that hung freely down his chest. He had only one eye in the middle of his face. His nails were very long and sharp. His eyelashes were so long they almost covered his single eye. His sight was so terrifying; the boy felt a shiver down his spine.

As he observed the surroundings more closely, he saw a palm tree in front of his house. Further up he saw an isolated house. Looking down the valley, he saw ten grass skirt plants well taken care of close to the house.

The old man looked at him sharply and told him not to go anyway near those items. There was coolness in the way he was speaking. It sounded like the boy was an intruder and not a grandson. The environment itself felt very unfriendly. Everything in there was staring back at him as if his presence was irritating. In his bones he felt that he was not welcome but did not express that to his mother. His whole process of the journey was for one thing and he had to complete that himself.

His mum left the next morning and he felt sadness like never before as he might not see her again.

In the days that followed, the boy was left to himself most of the time. Because of that, he had a lot of time to explore the land. Around the house, exploration was always hard as Granddad was always on guard. One fine morning, on one of the rarest of occasions, the Granddad called the young man in and told him he was going hunting. He instructed him not to go anyway near his isolated house and his grass skirt garden. The young man readily told him that he won't go anyway near them.

As soon as the old man was gone, the young man went straight to the isolated house. To his delight, the door was unsecured so he went inside. Once inside, the place was totally dark so he stood still while his eyes got used to the darkness. As his eyes got used to the darkness and more light was allowed through the open door, he gave a loud cry with what he saw.

The place was an open space and everywhere, as far as his eyes could reach, he saw human heads. After he got his energy back from the initial shock, he stepped closer and examined every face. His eleven brothers' faces were all lining up at one corner. With bitter tears in his eyes, he walked out of the hut and closed the door, leaving it just as it was closed by the owner.

He gathered all the bows, arrows and spears and hid them close to his sleeping corner and waited for the arrival of his Granddad.

Grandfather arrived but didn't enter his house. Instead, he started marching around his house proclaiming that his house was not in order. The boy came out of the house and shot him with his bow and arrow. The Grandfather shot back at him.

They fought until daybreak but nobody won. As the young man was about to give up, the old man told him not to touch his palm tree in front of the house. The young man, using his last ounce of strength, got his sharp spear and speared the palm tree down. At the fall of the palm tree, the old man fell as well. Furthermore, he cut down the ten grass skirts which saw the death of the ten girls including his mum.

He took the heads of his brothers and went straight to his home. Collecting as many salad leaves as possible, he laid the heads on them, nursing them till he brought them back to their usual selves.

After that they lived happily after.

The End.

Legends of the Mendi Valley

The Old Man was believed to be living beyond this mountain range.

Legend Three

POREAH HINN KOLUM

Once upon a time, two brothers called Porea Hinn and Porea Kolum, lived in a faraway land called 'Porea Por' in the Mendi Valley.

They were both very handsome and strong men who knew how to earn their living by working hard on the land. Their toil and sweat paid them well and so they lived happily.

They had big gardens that produced all kinds of good food, for they were very hard-working men and so they always had an abundance of food. They also looked after pigs and would kill one and mumu it once in a while.

Sadly, they didn't know anything of life beyond their own world, and so they both had no wives. Their single life was always full of things to do, from gardening to hunting, so it was a joyful life indeed.

However, every time that they mumued their special dinner, rain clouds would suddenly gather on the Noweah Mountains that towered above them, releasing rain which poured down on their hot mumu stones. They would struggle to build small shelters to protect their fire from being put out by the rain.

This went on for a while and the two men would sit down and wonder about it every time this happened. They then decided on a plan to find out the cause of all this rain.

One time Poreah Hinn told Poreah Kolum to gather things for their usual mumu. When this was going on, Poreah Hinn walked up the mountain to see if he could find out why it was always raining from this particular mountain during their mumu days.

After he climbed to the top of the mountain that towers over the land of Poreah Por, he hid himself under a canopy of trees nearby and waited. From where he sat, he could see his brother Poreah Kolum hurrying backward and forward as he got things ready for the mumu.

When at last he set the dry firewood on which the mumu stones sat on fire, thick smoke blew up from the mumu place into the air. As the smoke rose into the clear blue sky, Poreah Hinn could immediately feel the atmosphere changing. A quick gathering of heavy clouds from what was a very fine sky just minutes ago changed it from a bright sunny day to the sudden onset of darkness.

As he sat there wondering what was going on, he could feel the presence of someone else. He looked around quickly and he could see a creature sitting in a branch of a tree across where he was hiding. As he set his eyes on him, Poreah Hinn knew that person straight away; he was Berkesail, the forest god of that area. It was known that he lived in this part of the forest but no one has seen him with his naked eyes.

By now, Poreah Hinn was shaking uncontrollably, like leaves blown about by a strong wind. His heart was also beating very fast against his chest and his bladder had also given way to his fear.

As Poreah Hinn stared at the creature, Berkesail sat in all his glory on the branch, closely observing Poreah Kolum, who was busy going about his mumu.

Poreah Hinn recovered quickly from his initial shock and carefully studied this creature of a man. His whole body was equally divided into two. One side of his body was human while the other side had all sorts of plants growing all over him. Unbelievably he was half human and half plants, undergrowth and forest.

Not knowing that a human was hidden somewhere close to him, he gave a cough as if to clear his throat. In a deep and strong voice that almost scattered the leaves around him, he uttered the following words:

"Poreah Hinn and Poreah Kolum are cooking again in their land of Porea. These two brothers are so selfish, they don't know what sharing and caring and offering is", and spat a mouthful of huge saliva in their direction. As soon as he spat, rain poured down in huge drops. After that, he disappeared into the woods in the heavy rain.

Poreah Hinn climbed out of his hiding place and immediately ran down the mountain. He ran for his dear life, kicking stones and bumping into trees as he ran. He bumped into logs and rocks as he hurried down and ran all the way home as if Berkesail was in hot pursuit.

On arrival, he dropped down and took a breath and didn't talk for a while as he settled his breathing. After he was settled, he related everything that he had seen and heard to his brother.

After discussing with each other, they both decided that half of everything that was cooked in the Mumu was to be given to Berkesail, the god of the Mountain. That started with what was cooked on that day.

Every time they did their special meal of pig meat and other garden foods with hot stones, they would take Berkesail's share up the mountain and leave it on the spot where he was last seen sitting down. After that, it never rained again during their mumus.

This arrangement continued for a while. Both man and nature were at peace.

One night, while Poreah Hinn and Kolum were sleeping away, Berkesail sat contently on the very top of the rocky mountain known as Noweyah Manda. It was a very dark night. As he sat looking southward, he saw two traditional lights burning along the river. He decided to visit the source of these lights. On his arrival, he saw two very pretty girls hunting for frogs along the river bank.

He silently followed them to their house. The two girls, not knowing there was a third person in the house, dried their frogs over the fire for their next day's meal. Tiredness took over them and they fell asleep in total exhaustion.

After they were asleep, Berkesail lifted them up from their sleeping place on their sleeping mats and took them straight to Poreah Hinn and Kolum's house. He also took their personal belongings including the frogs that they had just killed, and left them inside the boys' house. He laid each sleeping girl beside each sleeping man. Nobody realised what was going on.

Early the next morning, the girls woke up to find two strange men sleeping beside them, and started screaming. The two men also woke up and the two girls accused the men of creeping into their beds to take advantage of them. The two men also accused the girls of doing the same thing to them. Suddenly, a heated argument broke out among them. In their great confusion, they all agreed to wait for the morning bird to sing its first song.

Poreah Hinn told the two girls, OLUMB is our morning bird that welcomes the daylight and announces the arrival of the new day to the sleeping people in this part of the land. In your lands it's the MONDIL that sings in the morning. If the OLUMB sings then we will know you two girls crept into our beds. However, if the MONDIL sings then we will know, it was us boys who came to you girls.

As they waited anxiously for the confirmation from the bird, it so happened that the OLUMB innocently sang away its beautiful morning songs. In total shame and confusion the two girls ran out of the house to return to their village. However, Berkesail used all his powers to block off all the tracks leading to their village, and the girls couldn't leave. Every track they tried was barricaded and they didn't know who was responsible.

Sadly, they stayed back with the two boys. Next morning the four of them woke up to find many pigs and kina shells neatly arranged around their house. Poreah Hinn and Poreah Kolum realised it was Berkesail who was thanking them by providing them wives as well as the bride prices. The two men with a thankful heart accepted the two women as their wives and paid their bride prices with the wealth provided by Berkesail, the Nature Man.

The two ladies accepted the men as their husbands and became mothers to all people living in that part of the land.

Berkesail continues to live contently in the forest til now.

The End.

Tuip Muar mountain, the home of Berkesial.
The very top seen here was where Berksial would sit and spy on Porea hin Kolum.

Legend Four

THE CHEATING CUSCUS

Once upon a time there lived a young man and his sister. The boy was handsome and his sister also was very beautiful.

They lived a happy life with an abundance of food that the land provided. Getting the supply of protein was not so hard either. The brother was such a skilful hunter, he would bring home cuscus and wild pigs that he had killed on his hunting trips.

Most of their gardening was attended to by the young girl while the boy took to hunting and clearing trees when they had to make new gardens. She would plant the best crops and they always had supplies of fresh garden food to eat. The boy, on return from his hunting trips, would bring the best cuscus home. They had supplies of local foods and animal protein to top it all up.

Their brother sister relationship was the best. Most afternoons they would sit around the fire place, relaxing in the warmth of the flame. They would share stories and other jokes and call it a night after enjoying each other's company. After all, they knew no other souls were near. The only human they ever knew was each other.

One fine day, the boy got himself prepared for his hunting trip while the girl got their breakfast of sweet potatoes ready. After a hurried breakfast they went their separate ways. The girl went for gardening while her brother walked up the track leading to the mountains, whistling happily to himself.

Reaching the very top of the mountain, he walked towards his secret cave. Before entering the cave, he looked around to make sure no one was looking. Once inside he removed his whole skin covering and placed it on top of a stone shelf. When he got out of the cave, he was a total stranger and with his bow and arrow firmly in his hands, went straight to do his hunting activities.

Meanwhile a cuscus was hiding nearby and saw everything that took place. Unfortunately, this cuscus was the most cunning out of all the cuscuses that lived in that forest. After watching the young man removing his skin and leave it behind to go hunting for his dinner, the cuscus also created plans at the back of his mind. The cunning cuscus watched him walk into the thick forest and decided to carry out his plan.

As soon as the young man disappeared, the cuscus jumped out of his hiding place and went straight to the entrance of the secret cave. Lifting the canopy of leaves out of the way, the cuscus crept in.

He quickly went for the boy's skin and covered himself with it. He now looked actually like the boy. Smiling wickedly to himself, he climbed out of the cave. Quickly making himself a blow pipe out of a small wild bamboo growing nearby, he also collected some hard wild seeds from a nearby tree. Whistling to himself, he walked down the valley and went straight to the boy's village.

He walked straight to the garden where the girl was busy working hard in the hot sun. The girl saw her brother coming towards her and wondered why he was home so early. She called over and asked him but, there was no answer. Instead he was coming straight at her and she wondered why the sudden change of mood. She started making small talk with him, but he made no reply. As she stared at him, she realised her brother's usual friendly face was absent, the face she was staring at now was expressionless and extremely dark and threatening. Raw fear had taken over her completely and she could feel herself shivering uncontrollably. Something was definitely not right with her brother. With a voice that was almost pleading, she asked for the last time what the problem really was.

Without a word he took out some round things out of his bag and fitted them into his blow pipe. This blow pipe too was a strange tool that she had never once seen her brother using for any purposes at all. Everything about her brother was strange this day.

Fitting the small bamboo pipe in his mouth, he blew the objects straight at the girl's breast. The pain was like the sting of a bee. She cried aloud in pain and begged him to stop, but he did not respond. Instead he blew more of those stinging seeds at her and she felt extreme pain from the stings like never before.

Now, in this part of the land, a girl's breast was the most sacred part of her body. For her only brother to blow strong objects at her breast was not allowed and this brought shame on the girl. As more of the objects were blown at her, she looked down to the ground she had been working all her life, in total shame and disbelief.

After reducing her to shame, the boy had disappeared. She hid behind a tree and cried till the sun went down. Her tears never stopped. Her eyelids were all swollen and her voice hoarse. She kept sobbing and sobbing until her eyes could cry no more.

The cuscus went straight back to the cave. After carefully replacing the boy's skin, he went on his way.

Without realising what had happened, the boy fitted his skin back on. He hurriedly took his bundle of cuscus and happily whistled his way home. Today's hunting had been exceptional. He had killed more than he ever had before and he was eager to show them to his one and only sister. So he took quick, happy steps down the valley as he rushed home with the day's bundles.

His sister always appreciated what he brought home and they would happily prepare their dinner together. Happily they would eat what was before them and happily they would share the afternoon together before going to their own bed to sleep. Hearing each other snore gently in their sleep was their comfort of the night. This time he looked forward to reaching home quickly and showing his always smiling sister all the bundles from the bush.

As he reached home, he felt something was not right. For one thing there was no smoke rising over their house and the house was cold. A fire was always alight in the house and the warmth would be welcoming. But today, the house was cold.

He quickly threw all the bundles down and went hurriedly to the garden. He searched for his sister everywhere but couldn't find her. His heart started beating very fast as he searched everywhere. As he came towards the big tree close to their garden, he saw his sister and ran over to her. His sister hung her head low and was crying.

Having him around made her worse and she started sobbing. He asked her over and over again what the problem was but she did not answer. At every question she cried more. When he moved closer to comfort her, she got up and ran away. He was so confused and worried, he did not know what to do.

In great disappointment, he walked back to the house. He wouldn't eat anything despite his hunger. All his precious bundles lay around idly as nobody attended to them. His sister didn't come into their house. He turned and twisted on his hard bed made of earth until day break.

Early in the morning he again asked his sister what really was the problem, but she kept crying in shame. Because he didn't know what the problem was, a great sorrow overtook him. His sister was unfair and mistreating him by not telling him of the events that brought her such shame and sorrow. He had been asking her over and over again but crying and hard sobbing was the only answer he got.

In frustration the young man selected their biggest pig and had it slaughtered. He had it mumued with hot stones with taro, banana and sweet potato. After it was cooked, he divided the cooked foods into two groups. He left his sister's share and loaded his share into a big net bag. He picked up his bow and arrow and started an unknown journey towards the sunrise.

When the sister realised what was happening, she quickly stuffed her share of cooked food into her bag and followed her brother. He was already gone so she went after him. The brother kept walking towards the sunrise until he came to a large tree. It was getting dark and rain was also pouring down so he found shelter under that tree.

The sister also, seeing that darkness was closing in on her, found shelter under a tree not far from her brother and waited for the rain to stop. Unfortunately, the rain didn't stop. It poured and poured until water filled every part of the ground that she was standing on.

As the rain continued to fall the whole night long, pools of water continued to rise until they reached their knees, then to their shoulders. It kept rising until water covered them both. They both were destroyed completely.

Early next morning, there was no sign of life but two big lakes had formed where the boy and girl had been standing. The two lakes remain til today.

The End.

Mountains where the boy went hunting.
The cheating cuscus lived in those mountains.

Legend Five

THE TALKING TARO

In a faraway land lived a mother and her pretty daughter. They lived very happily as the land provided all their daily needs.

One fine morning, as the sun rose over the mountains and the sky was very clear, they got their digging sticks and walked to their garden. Upon reaching their garden, they worked hard the whole day in the hot sun. They worked until evening and realised that darkness was quickly closing in on them, so they went home. As they entered their house, they were hungry, their fire had gone out and the fire place was cold.

Feeling cold and clammy, they tried to start the fire but in vain. As they looked around for any sign of smoke, they saw some rising in the next village. Leaving the old mother behind, the energetic daughter hurried over to the spot where they saw the fire burning. A huge welcoming fire had been built by someone. The warmth of the fire was so welcoming as its flame danced away into the evening sky. Its heat and glow gave warmth that seduced the young lady in her hunger, cold and tiredness.

She unwillingly turned away from the flame and quickly looked around for the owner of this eloquent fire. Unfortunately, he was nowhere to be found. Moving closer to the fireplace, she saw the hot ashes were mounted up as if something was being cooked under it. She quickly split the hot ashes apart and found a taro hidden under the hot fire. She quickly got it out of the fire.

Looking around again to make sure no one was watching, she put it into her net bag. After that she got a burning piece of wood from the fire and walked home happily. Upon reaching home, she quickly got the taro out and they ate it hungrily. After eating, they got their own fire going and happily sat around their fireplace, totally forgetting the events of the day.

Every time they had no fire burning in their house, the old woman would quickly send her daughter to get fire from the next village. The girl would happily run along and bring both fire and taro home. She and her mum would enjoy the taro for a long time.

As the days went by, the mother and daughter went about their daily duties, until one fine morning they heard a man calling for something from the distance. They didn't pay any attention to the call in the distance and went about preparing breakfast. However, in the silence of the cool morning, the voice in the distance was becoming persistent and powerful enough to make both mother and daughter stop to listen.

To their surprise, the powerful voice was coming closer and closer in the stillness of the cold morning air. As it kept coming closer and closer, the two women stared at each other. The whole environment stood still as if waiting in anticipation for something important that was about to happen.

Mother and daughter also stopped to listen to this very powerful voce calling out. Since they could not understand who the voice was calling out to, they waited for the voice to get clearer as it came closer.

By this time the person calling in the distance was now standing right outside their house. The ladies stood alone as his very presence filled their area.

He was a young and handsome man. His voice was like lightning that flashes across the sky. His teeth were so white the ladies could almost see themselves reflected in his teeth.

With every step he took, the whole earth shock. They had never seen a man like this one. Both ladies fixed their eyes on him and were quite unable to remove their gaze. His voice seemed to have the power to change their little world. Both women sensed that nothing could possibly compete with the power of his voice.

The strange young man, in an extremely loud voice that almost shook the foundation of the core of the earth, asked the two women if they had seen his taro. Both mother and daughter shook their head in unison to say they had no idea. They had never heard a voice like this in their lifetime. The voice lingered on forever in the still, morning air. They were by now shaking at the sound of his voice.

The owner of the voice too was so tall and muscular. His every footstep shock the very earth he stood on. His very presence filled up their surroundings. Besides his voice, his presence was an authority in itself.

He looked straight at them. The two ladies could not stand his stare, because he had eyes that could look straight into their innermost souls. The two ladies looked down and could feel themselves shaking uncontrollably like leaves blown away by a strong wind.

When the ladies denied ever stealing his taro, he got up immediately and started calling for Suwin and Pela, the names of his Taro. As he called for his precious cargo, something strange happened. To the uttermost surprise of the two ladies, a voice within the two ladies was heard responding to the call of the owner. From deep within the belly of the ladies rose an answering voice. "We are in here," the two taro responded.

The stranger turned around and stared at the two ladies, who stared back at him, full of fear. The younger woman by now was shivering uncontrollably under the scrutinising eyes of the man. His presence alone was powerful enough to melt them both. The man than asked the younger woman to marry him in return for his taro.

Without any further word or resistance, she surrendered to the owner of the taro.

They lived happily ever after.

The End

Taro cooked in hot ashes.

Legend Six

THE EVIL GRANDMOTHER

Once upon a time, in the Mendi Valley, lived a family consisting of a father, mother, a young boy and a young girl. They lived a simple and happy life. The mother did most of the garden activities while the father went hunting, so their meal was balanced with meat.

Most of the time the children would follow their father to the bush on his hunting trips. On those trips the boy was big enough to go hunting, while the girl looked for mushrooms, so they could make a contribution to the evening meal.

One fine day, the parents announced that they were attending a feast in a faraway land in the West. They stored up food and firewood for the two children and went off merrily on their way.

That very first evening after the parents had left, the two children sat around the fireplace feeling sad. They told each other sad tales that made their evening a sorrowful one. They both knew they missed their parents but nobody said that aloud. As the glow of their evening fire dimmed and the shadows of the evening became eerier, the night sky became darker and silence enveloped them. Suddenly there was a noise outside their door.

As they both turned their faces towards the door, they could not believe what they were seeing. Their grandmother stood in the doorway. The girl who was younger than the boy ran towards the door and hugged her tight. As for the boy, he felt a shiver run down his back, as he knew that his grandmother was dead. This one had to be her ghost.

Controlling his shivers, he smiled at his grandmother and welcomed her into the house. After the old woman settled herself around the fireplace, he started to plan how to keep his sister and himself safe from this ghost.

After a while, the young girl started yawning so the grandmother walked to the sleeping place and fixed the sleeping place with a mat that she had brought with her. She then lay down to rest and invited both of her grandchildren to share her bed.

The young man quickly refused to share her bed and told her they will sleep on their own bed. The young girl, however, disobeyed her brother and ran to her grandmother and lay down on her bed.

The young man, however, stayed awake all through the night and kept his fire burning until daybreak. Their grandmother was so unhappy that he kept the fire burning and told him so. After scolding the grandson for such behaviour at night, she went out of the house. She told him she would be coming back tonight and, as a good grandson, he should have respect for his grandmother. He should sleep with them instead of staying awake all through the night.

As soon as she was gone out of sight, the boy told his sister the fact that their grandmother was dead and so this visitor had to be her ghost. Because she was a ghost, she had come back to eat them tonight if they did not do anything.

After explaining all this to his younger sister, he started drilling into a post inside the house. He drilled until he created enough space for his sister and himself. In the evening they both fitted into the hole. After closing the hole up with a sticky tree gum, they hid inside. The boy then created a little spy hole through the seal to spy on the grandmother.

As they waited, the old woman walked into the house, after the midnight insects were heard. Upon entry, she immediately looked around for her grandchildren. When she couldn't locate them, she started calling for them. When there was no response, she started begging for them to come out of their hiding place as she was not here to harm them, but still there was no response.

She searched and searched until day break. Seeing daylight breaking across the sky, she ran into the forest. When she was out of sight, the two children crawled out of their hiding place, shivering from the cold morning as well as from the night's experience.

The big brother got to the fireplace and soon had the fire burning. The glow of the fire produced heat that was tranquilising, sedating the two young children to sleep. The boy reluctantly got up and collected sweet potatoes from the storage area and started cooking them for their breakfast, while his sister lay around the fireplace, unwilling to leave the heat of the fire.

Suddenly, there was a noise at the door. Both brother and sister looked towards the door and to their uttermost surprise, their grandmother appeared in the doorway. They both sat there without moving or even saying a word.

She walked confidently into the house as if she owned the place and made herself comfortable around the fire place, choosing to sit between the two children. As she sat there with an air of arrogance, the young boy studied her carefully. She was wrinkled up in most of her body including her face. Her eyes were sunken and lips dry. Her eyes were bloodshot and red.

As he studied further down her mouth, he could see huge amount of saliva flowing freely down the corner of her mouth. As she suddenly opened her mouth to give out a yawn, he realised that all her teeth were gone, except one which was on her upper left.

Suddenly she swung her thin neck in his direction, as if sensing all his observations, and looked right into his eyes. He quickly looked away but felt she had looked right into his soul. As she sat there, her face lying between her folded knees, she almost looked like a creature from another planet.

The atmosphere felt strange and heavy, almost suffocating him. As if reading his mind, the old woman turned to the younger girl and asked, in a kind and soft voice, "Where were you hiding in the night?"

Hearing the old woman asking this question, the young man became silent and stared at his sister so that he could signal her to not give away their hiding place. But his sister was not looking at him. Instead, she was looking in total admiration and respect at the old woman. From the way his sister was acting towards the old woman, he could see that she definitely was bewitched by her.

In desperation, the young man stood up to get his sister's attention but to no avail. Instead, she quickly told the old woman how her brother had hidden her against her will in the hole of the post of their house, drilled by her very own brother to hide them. The whole night that she had been hunting for them, they had been peeping and spying through the little space skilfully left by her brother when he covered the hole. Furthermore, she told her that she wanted to respond to her calls but the boy standing over there put his hand tightly over her mouth, so no voice came out of her mouth.

This time he was going to kill her. With a folded fist he rushed towards her, but the old woman stopped him with strength like that of steel. He wondered where such strength was drawn from, as she was very old. He promised himself to give his sister a bleeding mouth later!

The sister also told her grandmother that her brother told her that she was not their grandmother. She was a ghost imposter, posing as their grandmother, and was here to eat them. The young boy was so angry, he felt like wringing her neck for telling tales to the old woman, who he felt sure was a ghost or a witch. She was only here because she had seen their parents gone. If they were around, she wouldn't come. She was here with a wicked plan, he was sure of that.

The old woman, in her soft tone of voice, told the young girl, also turning to the boy, not to hide again, as she was not here to eat them, but to spend the night with them. She further added she was here to provide special comfort and peace like any grandmother. The young girl took every word she uttered and believed in what her grandmother was saying.

As for the young man, he didn't believe any of those words. He quickly made plans in his mind of what he would do when this evil woman arrived that night.

She told them not to hide again tonight but to wait for her, as she will be coming after midnight. Tonight will be their last night together as their parents would be arriving the next day, and she definitely did not want anything to interfere with their time together. As soon as the old woman left their house to return in the afternoon, the boy scolded the young girl for exposing their hiding place.

As the day passed by, the young man got his bow and arrows ready and hid them in one corner of the house. He got as many arrows as possible for they will become handy when he carried out his plans that night. Also, in preparation for the night, he gathered as many dry twigs and sticks as possible, filling one corner of the house. He also prepared enough water and food. Finally, he gathered hard rocks and left them with the arrows, so that he could use them as a weapon in the night too.

That afternoon he told his young sister to keep the fire burning all through the night as he would fight with the witch. If, for some reason, she let the fire go out, the witch would eat them up, as darkness was a friend to the witch. The girl feared being belted up by her brother and agreed to keep the fire going all through the night. He left some of the stones close to the fire place so they would get red hot.

The grandmother came in after midnight, with a rush of a strong wind that blew the curtains of banana leaves at the doorway. Her eyes were as red as the flame of the fire and her ears were standing up straight. Her face had changed from a loving, gentle grandmother's face to the totally strange face of a witch. She was looking around wickedly, as if looking for something in particular.

This time the young girl, who was sitting alone close to the fireplace, found herself sitting in a pool of her own urine after feeling her bladder give way. Her brother was right; she was a witch pretending to be their dead grandmother.

As the witch walked closer towards her, her eyes moving quickly from one corner to another corner of their house as if looking for someone, the young girl wanted to scream out in fear. But no word came to her mind. She sat there like a statue, unable to move. She tried to shout for help, but her throat was so paralysed, no word came out of her mouth.

The old woman tip-toed quietly towards her, eyeing her prey with eyes that had turned blood red. The young girl knew she had nowhere to run so she sat transfixed to the spot, wishing she had taken her brother's advice and not trusted the old woman too much by disclosing their hiding place. Now that she had no place to hide, she felt so exposed that she felt she would die out of fear before the witch even reached her. She should have taken her brother's advice.

Her thoughts were now racing towards her brother. Where was he? She had been too busy gathering dry twigs for the light in the night and didn't know where he went. Up until now, she had been too busy counting down the hours in anticipation of meeting her grandmother. She didn't realise he had slipped out. Right now she needed her brother like never before. She made up her mind to obey every one of his words right there and then. She watched in raw fear as the witch walked towards her.

As the witch got closer and closer, she lifted her right hand and, with clawed fingers, stretched her arm further out, directing long nails aimed straight at the girl's heart. Before the long, ugly fingernails touched the skin that covered her heart, a bow was heard striking from the corner of the house. An arrow came flying by and hit the witch in one of her eyes. The hand that was about to reach the young girl's heart withdrew quickly and went straight to her eye, pulling the arrow out as if it was just a needle prick.

This time, with strength she never knew she possessed, the girl screamed and screamed with all her might into the night. Her brother came out of his hiding place and shot another arrow straight into the witch's other eye at close range. The brief moment that the witch took to pull out that arrow was enough for the boy to come to the side of his younger sister, urging her with desperation in his voice to keep the fire burning, using the dry sticks and twigs that they had gathered during the day. If she failed on that, darkness would provide the perfect means for the witch to devour both of them.

This time the young girl took her brother's advice and provided light all through the night. She made a fire which provided the big, bright light for her brother to see to shoot hot arrows at the witch. The sharp arrows were shot at close range to her heart and other vital organs, but she didn't show any sign that she was wounded enough to fall. Instead, she brought out her own weapons and started shooting them at the young boy. Every weapon she threw at the boy missed him. He shouted to his sister to keep the light going on, because only by the light could they be saved. The fire with its light was their only hope.

The young girl realised that she had an important job at hand if they were to defeat the witch, so she diligently kept the fire burning with big bright lights. She kept her water container close to herself, so when she felt sleepy, she could drink and wash her sleepy eyes out.

They fought till daybreak. As the first light of day stretched across the sky, the dismayed witch gathered her things and disappeared into the forest. She had lost the war. The boy with the bow and arrow, and his sister with the bright light, had defeated the witch. She was a defeated foe and she was not returning.

The parents came home and they told them all the things that had happened during their absence. They were very grateful and proud that their son was very strong and innovative and was able to defeat the witch. They also were happy that their daughter supported her brother in keeping herself awake all through the night, so as to provide light for the war between the witch and the young man.

The End.

The witch grand-mother was thought to be living in this part of the valley

Legend Seven

THE TWO BROTHERS

Once upon a time, there lived two brothers namely Wuhai and Wapon. They were both bachelors. Wuhai was a gardener and Wapon was a good hunter. Hunting and gardening was what they did for their living. Wapon would go hunting during the day or in the moonlight at night and bring home fresh cuscus, wild pigs, or wild cassowary from his trips. Huwai would bring fresh garden produce which they would share together and make lovely meals for themselves.

One fine morning, Wapon went hunting as usual. He followed the traditional track leading uphill all the way to the mountain. As he reached the very top of the mountain after the long hard climb, he sat down to rest and take in the view, and the beauty that nature had to offer. Of all his hunting trips, this track was the hardest, but the best view comes from this hardest climb. Despite the difficulty of the climb due to the steep mountainside, he always looked forward to this trip. He always felt alive and awake when he reached the very top. He took a deep breath and sat on the top under the sky, feeling pretty much alive and well despite the walk. He felt in his bones that today would not be the same as previous trips. His spirit was light and there was joy in the air. He felt as if nature was walking so close to him to wash his spirit clean.

After rushing up to the highest peak to take in the unsuspecting beauty of the valleys, hills, fields, woods and the steep mountains, he now looked gleefully down and beyond the valley, where he could see Nature's powerful handywork in creation on display right now in its full glory. He was so thankful that he climbed up this far so he could enjoy and experience what wild nature had to offer, for it gave him a special kind of a peace that only these surroundings could offer.

The valley below was an endless green, giving him the best artistry nature had to offer. His own house was seen standing remotely in the endless green valley below. Graceful rivers flowed out of other ancient mountains, sitting peacefully between the green valleys. Beyond another blue mountain, a river was seen cutting through the rock with its persistent power. Yet on another mountain up north he saw a turbulent, silver waterfall, from which fog arose as waters from above hit the rocks below.

The rivers then rushed towards each other in the valley below, where they greeted each other and together danced far down towards some unknown lands. He wondered where all this water led to. He also wondered why those mighty rivers had been splashing down forever and yet never filled the land. These were rivers without end.

His eyes moved quickly from the valleys to the sky, which was a limitless blue and so clear today. Not a single cloud was to be found. Blue skies were smiling down at him from all directions. The sun had now risen above the Eastern Mountains and was shining straight at him. No matter how tall and proud the mountains stood, they did not block the sun. As the beautiful rays enveloped him in greetings, he felt as if he was truly home. Sadly, there was no one to share this beauty with but still he felt so much at home under the sky, with the cool air and huge, perfect, blue sky all around him.

Sitting at the top of the high mountain, he could see the beauty of the mountains showcasing creativity for him to uphold, and his heart leaped. Hearing melodies from the beautiful songs sung by all kinds of birds in the forest surrounding him was like music to his inner soul. A lovely breeze whispered back at him and filled his pounding heart with immense joy and pleasure.

As he looked back, tall and mighty trees stood together staring down at him. Through the big trees he could see no other paths and he took certain pleasure in the pathless woods. He wondered who planted the seeds that these mighty trees grew out of. Someone has revealed himself in all this handiwork but he didn't know who. For now, he looked up at the blue sky. A few white clouds had gathered in the distance. Recognising that fierce storms and strong winds had left the rustling leaves and rocks so undisturbed and unmoved, he felt contentment swelling up within him. He thought, what would be richer then to be witnessing this perfect gift of nature.

Falling back on his head, as if to take in more fresh breaths, he looked up at the sky and saw a few rolling clouds in the distance on this otherwise clear, blue-sky day. The amber clouds floated in the sky without a breath of air to move them around. Looking around he saw the silent forest looking back at him. He suddenly sat deep in thought at the wonders of creation.

For a brief moment he had forgotten about hunting for food for the house, and let his mind fly away at the wonders of the beauty of creation. As he sat silently on the top of the mountain taking in all the beauty of Mother Nature, he was content in it all. He truly felt his strength renewed and his hope restored.

Now his eyelids were getting heavier and started drooping. A sweet sleep overtook him and he fell into a deep trance. The smooth breeze from the valley below and the hypnotic silence had taken its toll.

In his deep but brief sleep, he heard a dog barking somewhere. It sounded as if the dog was calling him. He suddenly woke up and listened more intently. The dog's bark was not a dream at all. In the silence of the environment, the bark rose up clearly out of the valley where he was going hunting. Wapon was definitely sure nature was calling him for a higher duty.

He quickly gathered his hunting weapons and walked towards the sound of the dog's bark to investigate what was going on. As he came to a clearing in the valley, he hid himself near a big tree and silently observed the surroundings.

As he surveyed his surroundings, he saw a pig tied to a tree nearby. Then a huge brown dog appeared in the clearing. The dog gathered leaves, ferns, stones and firewood into one place, then walked straight to the big tree where Wapon was hiding. Wapon saw it was too late to run away, so he waited silently.

To his surprise, the dog talked like a human and asked him to follow it to the spot where he had gathered the things for a mumu. Wapon had no choice but silently obeyed the dog. The dog then directed Wapon to kill the pig that was tied to the tree. The dog also ordered him to take all the parts of the pig home, but asked Wapon to leave the heart behind for itself.

Wapon killed the pig and mumued it on the red-hot stones. After it was cooked, he removed the heart of the pig from its place and left it on top of a stone at a nearby cave, as he was directed by the dog. The dog then told him to come back after all the pork meat was finished.

Wapon hurried up the mountain and then rushed down the other side. This day was different. He did not have to hunt the whole day in the thick bush. Instead he had found a friend who had provided everything for him. He won't have to work hard to cook at home either. What he had in his bundles were all cooked and ready for eating. He was so excited, he rushed all the way home.

When he arrived, Wuhai brought out cooked sweet potatoes and they both enjoyed their meal. As they ate together, Wuhai wanted to know how his brother brought tamed cooked pork from the mountains. The other times it was usually wild pork and cooking was always done at their own home. Wapon wanted to keep this one secret to himself so told him misleading stories.

When the left-over pork was finished, Wapon went back to his friend the dog, and brought in more pork meat, except the heart. This went on for a while until one day, when Wuhai decided he wasn't eating any of the pork unless he was told the secret, and could go to the mountains to see for himself what really was taking place out there.

Wuhai insisted until Wapon could not take it anymore. So Wapon gave him directions and told him exactly how to handle everything. He especially told him that after slaughtering the pig, the heart was to be pulled out of its place and left on top of the stone shelf in the nearby cave. This was the most important part of all those activities in the bush.

Wuhai happily hurried up the mountain while Wapon took over his brother's job in the garden. As he tried to do some gardening, Wapon's heart did not settle. He could not concentrate on what he was doing as his mind kept going to the bush. He wondered if his brother was following all the advice and directions he was given.

As for Wuhai, he hurried up the mountain and down into the other side of the valley as directed. He did not stop to take in the beauty of the mountain top though. He rushed towards the cooking place instead. As he entered the clearance, he saw the dog and hurried towards it. However, when the dog saw the stranger, he asked what he was doing in his territory. Wuhai told him his friend stayed back and sent him to carry out the activities that he does with him.

The dog reluctantly walked towards him and Wuhai saw the pig tied to a tree. With the ferns, leaves and firewood gathered, the dog asked him to slaughter the pig and cook it. He could take all the pork home but must leave the heart for him in the usual place. Wuhai did the mumu but decided to keep every part of the pig, including the heart, for himself. He then got a huge stone and smashed the head of the dog, which was sleeping nearby. He carried his bundle and walked home.

Back at home, Wapon could not settle down. He walked in and out of the house with his heart beating wildly within his ribs. When Wuhai arrived at last, he met him in the doorway and asked how things have been. Wuhai told him to shut his mouth and eat first. Upon hearing such harsh words, Wapon almost fainted, but recovered quickly, took the load from his brother's shoulder and opened up the bundles.

To his greatest dismay, he saw the pig's heart still attached. He quickly turned around and asked why the part belonging to his friend the dog was found in the bundles. Wuhai declared he also wanted the heart for himself. The dog had had enough of all the heart, so this time he would have this special organ himself. Wapon could not take those words anymore. He went directly to his bed and tried to sleep, but sleep would not come easily. He tossed and turned until he fell asleep late into the night. In his dreams he heard the dog barking. It was a sad bark and was fading away in his dreams. He quickly got up from his sleep, only to find that daylight had already spread across the valley and the remaining darkness was quickly hiding from the onslaught of the light. The early morning animals were welcoming the day with all sorts of noise. In other times, he would lie awake and enjoy the noise as it sounded like a unified melody. However this morning was different, his heart was not silent and peaceful within himself as usual. He got his hunting weapons and rushed up the mountain.

As he rested on top of the mountain, golden sunrays had already brightened up the morning, bringing warmth into the frosty valley. He only took a few gulps of deep breath and walked hurriedly down into the valley of his friend. This part of the valley was yet to receive the sun so it was still cold and dull. His heart was also cold and empty as he approached the clearing. The familiar warmth was absent.

On any other morning, his friend the dog would rush towards him and greet him, but that also was absent. Things were not in order and his heart was sad. As he walked closer to their mumu place, he gave a loud cry. Lying there on the ground was his dog. His head has been smashed by a hard rock. He lifted him up and cried some more. After giving him a decent burial, he rushed up the mountain and ran down hill. As he reached home, Wuhai was nowhere to be found. He looked for him everywhere but could not find him, so he lay down to rest.

He woke up at the sound of footsteps nearby. He opened his eyes to look straight into a sharp spear pointed at his eyes. Wuhai was now pinning him down with the spear. Without any warning he speared Wapon through his eyes, against the hard earth.

After he had killed his brother, Wuhai collected his belongings and took off to other strange lands to settle. He could not work this part of the land. His brother's blood had spilled on it.

The End

The sun rising and sitting on the top of Mt Giluwe, the second highest mountain in PNG, viewed from the area in this legend.

Rolling clouds watched from the top of the mountain in this legend

Legend Eight

THE SECRET GROOM

Once upon a time in a small village lived a fine young man and his beautiful sister. Their parents had died a long time ago. They lived in a small hut at the foot of the mountain. Their daily needs were provided from the gardens and from hunting trips by the boy.

They lived in contentment for a long time until one fine day the boy announced his plans to travel, in the coming full moon. He was going for a pig kill ceremony in the far East. Before his travel, he made a big fence around their house, stored up enough food for his sister in a store house, and irrigated water into the fenced area as well.

Before he travelled the next day, he advised his sister not to leave their house. Everything that she needed for her daily living was all provided for within the fence, so she was not to leave the security of her dwelling place. With those words still ringing in the air, he walked down the valley, following the track that twisted and turned towards the rising sun. With a heavy heart, the sister watched until he was out of sight. She walked around restlessly all day wondering if her brother was going to be safe.

The young woman stayed indoors and within the boundaries of the fence. However, as each passing day turned into weeks, and weeks turned into months, the young woman grew restless. Her mind flew off to her gardens and fresh foods. She was also getting bored of eating stale stored food. So one fine morning she decided to disobey her brother and went to one of her gardens.

As she worked away in the hot sun, she thought she heard a dry stick snapping at a nearby bush. She stood still as she stared into the spot where the noise came from. To her surprise, a strikingly beautiful lady walked out of the bush. They greeted each other and the stranger said she was passing by and couldn't help noticing her working so hard in the hot sun, so she decided to help her.

With a thankful heart she welcomed the stranger and together they work in the hot sun. After the gardening was done, the young girl collected some foods from her garden. She wanted to send the stranger home, but the stranger wanted to spend the night with her and be on her way home next day. So, they spent the night together, enjoying each other's company.

Early the next day, the young girl collected the best food from her garden so the strange friend could take it to her house. The stranger asked the girl to help her carry the food half way to her own village.

Together, they walked in comfortable companionship until they come to the top of a hill. As they sat breathing in fresh air, looking down at the valley below, the stranger told the girl to go back to her village. Her own village was close by, so she would call her family to help carry the load.

The young girl pretended to walk away, but hid in the cleft of a rock she saw as they were walking by. She observed the strange girl, who stood in the clearing and called for her family members to come and help her. To her uttermost surprise, she heard a man's voice calling down instead. As she sat there silently, the young girl her age, who'd spent the night with her, changed into a very handsome young man right before her eyes. She was so scared she did not even make a noise.

Soon some pretty, energetic girls ran up the hill with joyful laughter. As they reached the top, they hugged their brother and started asking where he went during the night. As the girl watched from her hiding place, he playfully hugged them back and told them, he had been hunting. One of the girls asked why were there bags of garden foods instead of cuscus, if he was telling the truth. With a roar of laughter, he ran down the valley without answering her question. From below, he shouted back and told them that he will tell them the truth if they reach him before he reaches their house. The girls rushed forward to grab the bags of food and rushed to follow him, but he was gone with the wind. She wondered if they even reached him at all.

The girl quickly jumped out of her hiding place and ran all the way home, as if the devil himself was after her very own life. Safe in the sanctuary of her home, she recalled the entire recent event and wondered how this had happened. After all, she had even shared her very own bed without knowing he was a man. She suddenly shivered at the very thought of it, despite the bright sun and her body warmed from the run of her life.

In the days that followed, she continued with her gardening and other activities. On one such day, a little bird sat on her banana tree and sang its beautiful songs. As she paused to listen, the bird told her that the people who went for the feast, including her brother, would be arriving the next day. This message was sweet to her ears, especially after the most recent event. She missed her brother as he was gone a long time. She was now so happy that he was coming back the very next day. She would never be lonely again.

She quickly harvested the best food from her garden in preparation for his arrival. The whole day, she worked hard to get her house in order so that her brother, gone for so long, could be welcomed in comfort. She was hoping the day would go by quickly instead of taking too long for the darkness to arrive. She thought today was so long, the night wasn't coming quickly as it used to. She was restless until night fall. While lying on her bed, she thought about the stranger and decided not to tell her brother, as he might think she had been inviting strange people into their home. Let alone a strange girl who could turn herself into a young man! It gave her a shiver again just at the thought of it. It would be her secret for a lifetime.

She tossed and turned until daybreak. Early next morning, she had a bag of sweet potato cooked and went to wait on the road. As she sat on the road, she gave a piece of sweet potato to every single person coming from the East. Each one gave her a piece of pork and told her, her brother was coming behind them. He was bringing a lot of pork with Kolpa Pakhin. When she asked what Kolpa Pakhin was, she was told that Kolpa Pakhin was a woman witch. They should be arriving any time soon so wait and you will see for yourself, they said as they passed by. This totally crushed her spirit. She wanted to run away but her brother was arriving soon. She couldn't do anything but watched silently as if she was in a strange dream.

As her brother came into view, she sat at a distance and watched. Following behind him was a very strange woman, who walked with strange authority very close to her brother. Her brother had not changed so much, he was still looking very handsome. But the woman who followed very closely behind, as if she owned him, was a total stranger.

As she observed closely, she could see that the strange woman's head was irregularly shaped, with a horn growing straight up in the centre. Looking straight into the strange lady's face, she could see that she had only one eye, located on the centre of her face. Her nose was protruding out like the beak of a cassowary. Moving down to her chest, she could see two strange growths hanging down her neck. A shiver ran down her spine. This was no normal lady. She definitely was a witch and she wondered how on earth her brother teamed up with her.

As her brother slowly approached, she had a lot of questions for him. Before he greeted his sister, the strange woman following him came in between her brother and her, and introduced herself as Kolpa Pakhin, explaining that she was married to her brother. Kolpa Pakhin continued on, saying that the sister was no longer welcome in their house. She was also not allowed to go close to her husband and pulled him away from her.

The young girl realised that her brother was not defending her. So, with tears swelling up in her eyes, she collected her bag and walked away in total confusion. As she walked away in her confusion, she came across a creek with drinking water. A woman who was drinking water came out and greeted her. The young girl could not talk but just stared at her. The woman pointed at the direction of her house and told the girl to go there. She also explained that they were getting ready to go to a faraway land, and she should catch up with them so that she could also go with the family.

However, the girl decided not to go there, as the owner of that house had cheated her by hiding his true identity and approaching her as a girl. She hadn't forgiven him yet. However, his beauty had attracted her and while she wanted to investigate, her pride had kept her from doing so.

She continued to walk towards her own house. She realised, as she approached it, that there was a big barricade at the entrance of their gate, and she had no way of entering. She tried calling her brother over and over again, but her own voice was the only human voice in the still, cold air. There was no answer to her call.

With tears in her eyes, she turned back to the way she had come. The only other human she had ever known was the stranger who appeared to her as a girl and later became a boy. She had no choice but to go to his house. Walking quickly down the valley towards his house, she focused on the road ahead, as the sun was quickly setting and soon darkness would cover the valley.

When she arrived at the house, no other person was to be seen. All had gone, just like the strange woman had told her. She threw her bag on the ground and sat close to their mumu place, sobbing loud with uncontrollable tears. As she sat there with hot tears rolling down her face, a rat appeared.

The rat told the girl that all in the family had gone and that she was too late now to join them. No amount of crying will bring the boy back. At that, the girl cried more. The rat waited till she stopped to wipe away her tears. It told her that the boy asked him to bring her when she changed her mind and came back to him. The girl was now ready to do anything the rat told her to do, as long as it took her to the handsome boy. The rat then told her to grip his tail. She had no hope and no choice but to hold onto the rat's tail. As the rat turned around, a very tall palm tree stood in front of them.

The rat told her to be confident and hang onto his tail until they reached the top of this special tree, which had just appeared from nowhere. She did as she was told, and the rat started to climb the tree slowly. He climbed and climbed, but there seemed to be no end to this tree. The rat seemed to know the path, so the young girl rested in comfort as he moved upward and onward. It took such a long time. When the young girl looked down, the whole earth had disappeared. It seemed like she was riding on the white clouds. She could not believe what was happening to her but, for now, she would put her trust in the rat which had brought her this far.

As they finally reached the top, it looked as if the tree had reached the heavens. It was not so easy for the girl to move over to the top. As she looked up, an old ancient looking man appeared and pulled her over to his side. She turned and looked down to thank the rat, but it had disappeared. She sadly turned around to face the man who, with an authoritative voice, ordered her to follow him.

As she walked closely behind, she observed that she was in a totally strange land. This land was above their earth which she had left behind. She also noted that, while it was dark below, the bright lights of this land were different. There was a certain comfort in this land that no words could express. He led her to a house and told her to go inside. In the house there were so many beautiful young ladies. Nobody seemed to take notice of her entrance or her presence. They were all talking and playing with each other.

She didn't know what to do and was about to approach one of the girls when an old woman walked towards her. She then asked her if she was the woman that the owner of the house was checking on. The young girl nodded her head to say yes. Looking her up and down, she abruptly took the girl to a room and told her to settle down. She then told her that the young boy had married all those women.

She looked down to the ground in total sadness, because the boy had married some other beautiful ladies already. She was too late, all because she went to see if her brother would let her into their house. But it was never meant to be. He and his witch of a wife had locked her out. If only she had taken the advice of the lady who she met at the side of the creek, she would have been the one he married.

As she tried her best to put her past behind her, she sat in total silence. She can't go back as she had come too far; surely there was no way back to earth. She felt she was now too far from her brother and his totally strange wife. Even if she went back, she had no home to go to, so she might as well stay here.

As she sat there, she heard a deep sweet voice behind her and turned around. Standing there staring down at her with such wide and loving eyes was the boy. Seeing him so close, she thought he looked so handsome. He was so tall and well-built. Her heart came to a standstill. She could not breathe. Why did she not come quickly when she was given the chance?

"So, you are here at last," he tormented her. "I thought you didn't want me. The time had come for me to come to this forever land, so I got myself other beautiful girls who wanted to come with me. And now you are here. So what brought you here?" At this the young girl wept.

"How could I know that you were a man? How could I even know you don't belong to the earth below?" she lamented. "I had my own issues and I arrived late. How could I even know you had other beautiful girls who were coming after you? I'm only here because of a rat who brought me here. Please if you do not want to marry me, leave me in peace because I have had enough for the day and can't take anymore."

At that he told her, he had sent the rat to bring her up to where he was because he saw the situation she was in. "Your brother bringing a witch for a wife, the witch throwing you out of your own house, you going to my house when I had already taken off, it was also painful for me," he said. "I couldn't stand it."

"You see, I came to you as a total stranger in your garden because I loved you," the boy continued. "I knew you were hiding in the rock behind me that day. You left me with the bag of food. That's why I revealed myself, so that you would know that you had a visit from a man."

"I was going to come back for regular visits, but I saw you were so angry so I couldn't come back. However, I did send my sister to direct you to my house because I saw your brother had mistreated you, but you refused to come. The time for my wedding and time for me to leave the earth and come to my forever land had arrived, so I had to rush off."

"I only sent the rat to bring you here because my love for you was never ending and unconditional," continued the boy. "I couldn't stop loving you. I couldn't stop wishing for you to come to this land with me. Therefore I had to plan a rescue mission, and it was successful. I sent the helper down so it would bring you up. He was the only one who knew the way. I knew it would be a fairly difficult ride up the palm tree, but the most important thing is you are here safely. So welcome home."

On that note, he hugged her and married her. That night there was a big celebration in the forever land. They lived happily ever, after becoming the parents to all the Yeki (angels) above.

The End.

She was taken up into the clouds and became the mother of the Yekis.

Legend Nine

WAR WITH THE GIANTS

Once upon a time a young man, a young woman and their dog lived in the Mendi Valley. The dog was called Tala hin. The boy and Tala hin would go hunting and bring fresh cuscus home as a contribution to their meal.

One day on such a hunting trip, Talal hin got lost in the mountains and the boy came home alone. Brother and sister refused to eat as they were both were so sad for their dog. Early next morning, to their great surprise, the dog was heard barking outside. They both rushed out to greet it. As they hugged him, the dog struggled out of their welcoming arms and led them over to his sleeping place. A young cassowary was sleeping there comfortably. So he had brought a friend home. They gladly named him Tuk Ten Piu. The cassowary became part of their family, and all lived happily together.

One fine, bright sunny day, they all decided to go gardening. As they got busy with the garden activities, Tala hin gave a few quick barks, constantly pointing to the southern end of their land. As they all looked in that direction, they saw a dark form in the distance. This dark form looked evil. As they watched in total silence, the dark form slowly came towards them.

Tala hin and Tuk Ten Piu quickly got out of their position and told the two people to stay and watch, while they hid on the road to see what this dark thing was. Without waiting for a reply, they ran all the way to the main road.

As the dark form approached them, the hidden Tuk Ten Piu and Tala hin could feel the earth trembling under the footsteps of this dark form, which was fast approaching their hiding place. Their surroundings were getting darker despite the bright sun still hanging down in the middle of the sky. The clear blue sky had quickly gone into hiding behind the thick dark clouds that had begun to darken the sky.

The surroundings had gone so quiet, as if sensing the approach of this total stranger, who was walking forward very slowly. Tala hin and Tuk Ten Piu observed the approaching creature with real terror in their hearts. The creature was so tall it reached to the tree tops, and its body occupied the track it was walking on. At closer range they could see two horns growing in the middle of its large head, and an eye in the middle of its big round face.

Both Tala hin and Tuk Ten Piu knew that if they allowed it to pass through, their human friends would be in serious trouble. Without thinking, Tala hin went for its heals while Tu Ten Piu went for the eye of the unsuspecting giant. Their attack was so sudden, so fast and furious, the giant had no time to readjust itself and so down it fell. At his fall the whole earth experienced a mighty last shock and the sky thundered loudly. Then rain suddenly poured down. The two friends ran all the way home with their great news. There was great celebration in the home of the four friends that evening.

The next morning, the sky was blue and clear and the sun had risen earlier than usual. The four friends quickly had their breakfast of roasted sweet potatoes and went to work in their garden. Tala hin the dog, as usual, sat lazily around.

As the sun got hotter, the dog sat under the shade of a big tree and dreamed of a better dinner than what he had for breakfast that morning.

No sooner had he lazily closed his eyes than he sat up straight, momentarily forgetting dinner. Tala hin could not believe his eyes. He rubbed them hard as if to make sure he was not just daydreaming. However, it was not a dream at all. He could see dark forms in the distance coming towards them. He screamed at his friends to look at the very strange, dark forms in the distance. They seemed to be slowly moving towards them.

All three dropped their working tools and turned their heads towards the direction Tala hin was indicating. The giants were now back for revenge. Tala hin and Tuk Ten Piu told the young boy and girl to hide in a cave while they went and made war with the giants. Without waiting to hear back and get a reply, they quickly ran down the track towards the river that separates their village from the next.

The river was huge and flowing fast, with a rope bridge that linked the two villages together. They rushed all the way to the river and ran across the rope bridge. There was a cave in a rock under the bridge on the other side. They hid themselves in the cleft of the rock and planned their attack on the approaching enemies. As they sat close together, as if to comfort each other, Tuk Ten Piu decided he would go for the eyes of every giant while Tala hin would go for their heels. They had shared their plan and now they sat quietly in great anticipation of the coming battle.

As they sat in the cleft of the rock listening intently, they felt a slight tremor of the earth and they knew, the giants were close now. A sudden fear overtook Tuk Ten Piu but, she did not show that she was scared. She put on a brave face instead, and waited.

The bridge was seen swinging freely from the tremors. The trees danced from the movement of the earth from every step the huge approaching giants took. As they came closer to the bridge, the two friends could see they were countless in number. All looked the same as the one they had killed yesterday.

When the first giant approached the bridge, Tala hin rushed out of his hiding place and went straight for the giant's heels, while Tuk Ten Piu went for the eyes. The two friends were too fast for the huge giants. They fought them until they killed them all. By then it was getting dark, so they ran all the way home and related all their experiences to their human friends. The boy and the girl were so happy; they put up a huge party for them that night.

Tala hin and Tuk Ten Piu lived a happy and contented life until one day they went hunting in the mountains with the boy. After the day of hunting was over, they happily headed home whistling, with their bundles for a special dinner of cuscus.

As they approached home, they saw no smoke coming out of their house as was usual, and the atmosphere was cold, as if nobody had ever lived there. They threw their bundles off their shoulders and all three started calling for the girl, but there was no answer. They searched the whole place over and over, but there was no one to be found. As they sat around the fireplace, all lost in their own thoughts, nobody seemed to want to talk. At last, the dog spoke out what was in all their minds… the giants had come and taken the girl away. Sadly, they nodded their heads quietly and fell asleep, just where they were sitting with their dinner. Tuk Ten Piu cried her eyes out before she fell into a deep, deep sleep.

Each passing day, they would mourn for their sister and refused to eat or work, until one day Tala hin and Tuk Ten Piu decided to go and look for her. The young man refused to let them go but they resolutely decided that they were going on that trip. They told him, "If we come back safely from this trip, you will see smoke on top of the mountain that separates the giant valley from our valley as a signal. If you have not seen any smoke rising within the next few days then, it would be a message to you that we have all been devoured by the enemy giants."

As they started out on this very dangerous trip, they fondly hugged their friend, who wept openly for them. After bidding him farewell, they travelled down following the mighty Lai River. They travelled and travelled until they came to the border between the giant's and human's valley.

As they entered the giant's valley, they didn't take the common tracks but decided to walk through the bush, so as to hide themselves from any observers. They walked up hills and down valleys, also crossing fast flowing rivers, until they came to a clearing on top of the hill overlooking the village of the giants.

As they sat on the top overlooking the place, they could see giants going about their activities. In a nearby garden, normal women were making gardens. They were women captured by the giants and brought to their village as slaves. They will then be killed by the giants one day at a time for their meals.

As they slowly walked towards the gardens, they could see their sister working among the group of young girls. They both gave a sigh of relief, for their sister was still alive.

Tala hin told Tuk Ten Piu to wait in the nearby bushes, while he approached the girl acting like a dog from the area. The dog then approached the sister without anybody suspecting him. When the girl saw that it was Tala hin, she almost gave a cry of joy but controlled herself and played with the dog instead. Speaking into his ears, the girl asked how he had come this far? Tala hin also whispered to her and told her that Tuk Ten Piu was also hiding nearby. She needed to go with them now as they had come to rescue her.

For now they were not safe, because everyone in this part of the land are giants and carnivorous. She then showed Tala hin the house where they were living, and told them that they will escape in the night, after setting fire to their house so the giants won't follow them. Meanwhile they were to remain in the bushes waiting for night to approach. Tala hin walked back to the bushes and told Tuk Ten Piu all that was said. They sat quietly, for the atmosphere was infused with danger.

The women now walked back to their house, not knowing the two friends of one of their members were hiding nearby. Once it was dark, the two friends walked quietly towards the giants' house. As they approached, they could hear the giants' very loud snoring.

The girl met them at the end of the village, as was planned, and they all walked stealthily toward the man-eating giants' dwelling place. Using strong bush vines that the girl had gathered, the three friends tied the vines to big logs, forming a barricade to the entrance of the giants' house. The girl had counted and was sure all were inside and safely sleeping.

After securing the entrances, they set fire to the building and ran up the hill towards their own side of the valley. Luckily, a full moon was up and providing light for them. Reaching the top of the hill, they all sat down for a rest. They could hear shouts from the burning giants coming from deep down the valley. They didn't stay long enough to hear more as they had to cross over to their side of the valley before the moon went into hiding again.

When they reached their side of the valley, daybreak was already approaching. They set a big fire on the mountain as they said they would if they were coming home safely. The boy, who was watching the mountain day and night, saw the fire in the mountain early in the morning, and was overcome with joy. He knew what that meant, that were all coming home safely.

As the weary travellers reached home, they discovered the young man had already prepared a special dinner for them. They once again enjoyed each other's company and enjoyed the party. They then lived happily ever after.

The End.

Legends of the Mendi Valley

The blue mountain in the distance was believed to be the border between the giants and people.

Legend Ten

THE CALLING OF THE RISING SMOKE

Once upon a time, a mother and her daughter lived in the northern end of the Mendi Valley. They lived in their hut with the land providing for their daily needs.

No other humans lived in that part of the land. They were the only human beings living in the land. Their lives were sometimes lonely, and they would look for ways to look for other people, but they could not find anybody.

To forget their loneliness, they would commit all their time to gardening each day. As a result, their gardens were filled with the best sweet potatoes, taros, sugar cane, ginger, and so on. The best of all garden produce was found in their gardens. They were always content with what they had.

A graceful river flowed beside their gardens. It was always clean despite heavy rains. It produced water cress as white and as fresh as the river itself. Sometimes they would sit beside the river and it would tranquilise them to sleep. They were thankful Mother Nature had provided them with comfort from nature itself.

One bright sunny day, as they sat down under a tree to rest from their hard work, they looked up to the mountains towering high above them. To both of their surprise, something strange was visible rising towards the sky. A fine column of smoke was seen rising innocently into the air. Both women sat up straight to see this strange thing unfolding right before their eyes.

As they sat there staring into the high Blue Mountains, both mother and daughter had all sorts of questions going through their minds. They both decided that, if there was smoke rising at the foot of Bee Wiri Mountain, there has to be someone living there, and they must go and look for that someone.

For now it was already getting late, so they went to their house and prepared for the encroaching darkness. As they sat around the fireplace enjoying their roasted sweet potatoes, the topic of their conversation was the rising smoke. They had questions about who that person was, was he human or a demon? If human, was it a girl, boy, man or a woman? In their excitement, they talked late into the night and stopped only when their eyelids were heavy with sleep. Finally, they fell asleep in the early hours of the morning.

Despite their late night, both women were fully awake at the first song of the early morning bird. They quickly got the fire going and prepared their breakfast. After a light breakfast, they both went out to watch the sun rise into the still, early morning air. As the sun warmed everything up, they looked up towards the Bee Wiri Mountains that stood so tall, towering above them and rising up towards the heavens. And there, rising up very high into the clear blue sky, was the fine, silver column of smoke.

As they stared in total amazement, the smoke seemed to change its direction, going upward and then turning towards the west, as if calling them to the source of the fire. Now, the ladies were sure, the smoke that goes up forever was changing direction to ask them to go to the mountains, but how could they go up there? There was no road leading up towards those mountains.

In the days that followed, the smoke in the Blue Mountains continued. The women felt they were being invited by this wonder of nature but, despite all their attempts to look for any tracks that would lead up there, they could not find a way leading them to the rising smoke.

As the days came and went, the two women searched for a way to go to the Bee Wiri Mountain of smoke, but were unsuccessful. One day they came home weary from the search and sat watching the river gracefully flowing down. As they cooled themselves with the fresh water, the girl jumped up and excitedly said something. Her mother asked her to settle down and talk properly.

"Can't you see?" she screamed. "This river has its source at the Bee Wiri Mountains." She spoke between breaths, pointing to the river.

"So, what's the point," the mother answered lazily. The next instant she too jumped up and down as the reality hit her. They could follow the river to its source and find the owner of the smoke too.

They slowly waded up the clear river. As they got closer to the mountain, they could see fresh, healthy watercress growing everywhere. They told each other they would pick them on the way for dinner. As they got closer to the smoke, they could see it rising above the mountains and disappearing into the sky, mingling around with the thick clouds above, which were threatening to send down rain.

As they moved forward, they suddenly come to a halt, for the river track had a dead end. To their great dismay, high rocks formed a barricade to the lands beyond. As they looked around the tall rocks that stood as a fence blocking them, they struggled to find a way past. It was as if nature had meant to keep any intruder out of its own creation beyond the rock fence.

Clean, fresh water flushed out of the rocks and flowed down to the ground, continuing downstream the way they had come. The river close to their garden was sourced by a waterfall that came crashing down at their feet. As part of the waterfall hit their feet, already numb from their arduous walk through the water, pain filled their toes. It was as if the water and its surrounding environment did not welcome their presence.

Despite the hostility of the surroundings, mother and daughter started looking for a way to climb up the rockface so they could reach into the lands beyond. However, the rock was so high, any attempts to climb it would be pure suicide. There was really no way up. Nature had built its fence to keep them out, they were sure of that.

They both cried in pain from their painful toes. In dismay, they realised this was another search in vain. As they sat there crying, all of a sudden a figure appeared above the rocks with something in his hands. Without looking down, he threw down what was in his hands and disappeared as quickly as he had come. Pig's intestines landed in front of the two women.

The two women stared up into the empty space as if they had just seen a ghost. No, it was not a ghost. It had to be real, because right in front of them was the thing that he threw down. With some more tears, they cleaned the intestines and took them home with the watercress, and prepared dinner. They didn't talk much, nor did they enjoy their dinner. They went straight to bed and fell into a deep sleep.

The next morning, they were both awake early as usual and had a quick breakfast. They walked up the river again and did a thorough search for a way that would lead up to the inviting smoke and its owner, but there was no way up at all. As they looked up wishfully, the stranger from above appeared suddenly again and threw more pig's intestines down at them, before disappearing into the forest. Greatly disappointed, the two women returned home with the pig's intestine and watercress. Once again they had their dinner and slept without saying much. This went on for some time until one fine day the two women went up the river again.

Legends of the Mendi Valley

When they reached the waterfall, they sat at their usual spot and stared up into the space where the stranger would appear, so they could get a quick glimpse of him before he disappeared. They were concentrating so hard looking up that they did not notice a visitor in their mist.

Standing between them was a wallaby, who asked them why they were here every day just to stare at the very spot that they were staring at right now. Reluctantly, they started to relate their story to the wallaby from the beginning. The wallaby felt so sorry for them. She told them to climb into her pouch and she would bring them up to their most desired destination.

After the women made their way into the pouch, the wallaby found her way up the rockface and dropped them beside a big tree. She then advised them to hide in the hollow of the tree and observe the activities that go on around them. She asked them not to talk or make any move but told them to observe until the man made his last move, then one of them can follow him. After giving that advice, she was gone.

From where they sat, they could see the source of smoke and its owner clearly. The owner of the smoke was a handsome man who was making a fire to mumu his pig. As he set about his cooking preparation, he got so busy he didn't notice the two ladies sitting nearby, spying in on him. When his pork and other food stuffs were in the mumu, he ran down to the top of the rocks and threw the pig's intestines, before running back again. The man was so tall and built so handsome that the two ladies were speechless. They were sure there was no one like this figure anywhere in the whole world. He was so breathtaking. When he walked, the whole earth shock and when he laughed, lightning flashed across the sky. He was one of a kind.

After waiting for a while, he removed his mumu and put everything into a net bag. He lifted the bag onto his shoulders and walked towards the top of the water fall. As the two ladies watched silently, he walked into a pool of water collected on top of the rock, which seemed to be the source of the river that flowed beside their garden on their side of the world.

Without thinking, the girl jumped up and collected a strong bush vine nearby. She told her mum to tie one end to her right leg and hold onto the other end. She would follow the man into the round pool. If her life was in danger, she would move the rope so the mother could quickly pull her back.

Having done that, she jumped into the pool. As she swam down, she didn't have far to swim. Right before her was a beautiful village. The beauty of it took her breath away. There was only one house in the centre of the village and no one to be seen. She walked to a nearby tree close to the house and hid behind it.

She heard a noise and as she looked in that direction, to her uttermost surprise, firewood dropped from the sky. Then came down net bags of taro and sweet potato. The last to fall was the young man, who was secretly often in her thoughts. As she stared in amazement, he quickly got his stone axe and chopped the firewood. As he chopped away in the still air, a piece of wood flew into the air and landed in the foot of the girl who was hiding.

With a heavy sigh, he walked towards his firewood to collect it. Realising what was happening, she pulled the piece of firewood out of her foot and threw it away nearby. He quickly picked it up and walked back. The girl still hiding gave a sigh of relief!

Suddenly, the young man stopped and turned back. His firewood had blood on it and he needed to check, as firewood doesn't bleed when chopped. As he walked towards her, the girl realised it was too late to run away or even hide properly, she could only stare at him with frightened eyes. Without saying anything, the young man pulled her by the arm and took her to his house, where he gave her a decent meal and asked her what she was doing here, and which road she had come from.

The young girl had no choice but to relate all the stories from the beginning to the end. He sat there listening in silence. After she had completed telling her tale, the young man told her to lie down next to him, as he had only one bed. As she lay next to the stranger in a strange place, she could not get to sleep. She lay there staring into the dark. In the early hours of the morning, she looked across to where the young man was lying. She could not believe what she was seeing, for lying on the bed next to her was a very large snake.

The first thought that came to her mind was to jump up and run away, but something calmed her down. After all, if she ran away, where and to whom could she go to? Life with her mother was boring and she had felt somewhat comfortable lying close to this stranger. With that in mind, she grabbed the snake and held tightly onto it. The snake tried escaping but the girl would not let it go. Suddenly the snake turned into a small tree full of thorns. This she also grabbed and held onto tightly, regardless of its prickles.

The tree then turned into a wild pig, which she hung onto desperately until the first song of the morning bird. The wild pig then turned into the handsome young man that he was. As she hung onto him, he asked her to wish for anything and it would be granted immediately. She answered that all she wanted was his company and presence. She did not wish for any other thing.

The young man then granted her wish. They went to pick up her mother, who was waiting patiently for the return of her daughter. The rope that was tied to her leg was removed. The young man brought the young girl back to her mother, who readily accepted him as her daughter's husband.

They lived happily ever after.

The End.

Smoke would rise from the foot of the mountain

PART B

EVIDENCE OF YAWEH'S FOOTPRINT IN THE TEN LEGENDS

*L*egend was used by the people of the Mendi Valley in the Southern Highlands of Papua New Guinea to convey moral lessons, and present useful information and everyday life lessons in an easy way for the common people to understand. The Legends told also gave the audience directions on how they should behave in life for the present and future, born as they were from historical events and real life moments that became part of our collective cultural context. The people of the valley also believe that, at their core, Legends contain a seed of hidden truth, unlike myths.

Most importantly, within the fabric of each world's culture are embedded traditions that point the way to the Gospel message. God in His Greatness planted evidence of Himself throughout so many cultures of the world, for it was God's original plan to draw all mankind to Himself.

After the fall of Eve and Adam in the Garden of Eden, God's purpose throughout the Scriptures and through history was to bring all people to Himself by grace through his Son on the cross. How did God work in history apart from Israel to save sinners? God in His Master plan has preserved remnant memories of Himself embedded in each culture, preparing the Gentiles everywhere for the Good News of the saving grace of Jesus His son.

Likewise, for the children of the Mendi valley, God in His kindness has left traces of truths hidden within their traditional legends that point to the Gospel of Christ Jesus. Almost all cultures and oral traditions of the people of Mendi valley give startling evidence of the one true God of Israel.

The common misconception that people of tribal nations or areas are totally lost without the Gospel, fumbling around in the darkness, is not quite true. For as the Scripture says;

> From one human being, he created all races of people and made them live throughout the whole earth. He himself fixed beforehand the exact times and the limit of the places where they would live. He did this so that they would look for Him and perhaps find Him as they felt around for Him. Yet God is actually not far from any one of us;
>
> Acts 17:26-28 [GNT]

Remarkably, remote pagan worshippers nevertheless possessed and eerily preserved traces of the gospel message down through the generations until missionaries arrived with the good news of the Gospel. When the missionaries did arrive, the people readily and happily embraced the salvation through Jesus Christ. God has left a trace of Himself in the hearts of people throughout history and cultures. God is big enough to show this world that He existed within their cultures.

The Almighty God of Israel also embedded a nugget of truth in the legends told in Part One of this book. These legends were handed down in the most sacred and most loving way possible from generation to generation, and are now told over and over again. Parts of these legends are sometimes used as an example by local Preachers to Preach the Gospel today as well.

The children of Mendi valley who just got exposed to the outside world not so long ago (1950s) were blessed. God had prepared their hearts in their own pagan cultures, enabling them to understand the meaning of the Gospel. What are the wonderful acts of God? His wisdom is displayed by preparing the Gospel for certain tribes and people in this extraordinary way, so evidence of belief can be provided for the one True God in the legends of the people of this part of the land.

In the following chapters, the legends in Part One have been discussed in view of the word of God. Scriptures have been identified as proof that God had truly planted His word among the cultures of this part of the world, that is, the cultures of the people of the Mendi Valley.

Legends of the Mendi Valley

Footprint One

TAR MAN PAPLIN & IP TEKES PIU

*I*n this legend, the all-powerful call of the melodies of the Kundu drum is identified as the call of wisdom. This call was a call to worship the maker of Heaven and Earth.

A. The Call of Wisdom

All people in all corners of the world are indeed drawn to wisdom as there is something profound about wisdom. Everyone seems to understand instinctively that by wisdom, one will gain direction and other solutions in life's situations. That indeed is precious and so it's a treasure. True wisdom is a gift that comes from God and it must be well sought after and be cultivated (Proverbs 2:6, James 1:5).

Wisdom is loving with an understanding heart. It is also humble and discerning. It is pure and permanent. Wisdom is the principal thing needed to grow up and be a responsible person. It goes deeper than mental abilities. It surely is a fountain of living waters and the one who finds wisdom finds life.

The book of Proverbs urges us many times and in various ways to get wisdom, to be able to live in the blessings it brings.

Proverbs 8:1-31 [GNT] for instance:

Listen! Wisdom is calling out.

Reason is making herself heard.

On the hilltops near the road and at the crossroads she stands.

At the entrance of the city, beside the gates, she calls;

"I appeal to all of you; I call to everyone on earth.

Are you immature? Learn to be mature.

Are you foolish? Learn to have sense.

Listen to my excellent words; all I tell you is right.

What I say is the truth; lies are hateful to me.

Everything I say is true; nothing is false or misleading.

To those with insight, it is all clear; to the well-informed, it is all plain.

Choose my instruction instead of silver; chose knowledge rather than the finest gold.

"I am Wisdom, I am better than jewels; nothing you want can compare with me.

I am Wisdom and I have insight; and I have knowledge and sound judgement.

To honour the Lord is to hate evil; I hate pride and arrogance, evil ways and false words.

I make plans and carry them out.

I have understanding, and I am strong.

I help Kings to govern and rulers to make good laws.

Every ruler on earth governs with my help, officials and nobles alike.

I love those who love me; whoever looks for me can find me.

I have riches and honour to give, prosperity and success.

What you get from me is better than the finest gold, better than the purest silver.

I walk the way of righteousness; I follow the paths of justice, giving wealth to those who love me, filling their houses with treasures.

> The Lord created me first of all, the first of his works, long ago.
>
> I was made in the very beginning, at the first, before the world began.
>
> I was born before the oceans, when there were no springs of water.
>
> I was born before the mountains, before the hills were set in place, before God made the earth and its fields or even the first handful of soil.
>
> I was there when he set the sky in place, when he stretched the horizon across the ocean, when he placed the clouds in the sky, when he opened the springs of the ocean and ordered the waters to rise no further than he said.
>
> I was there when he laid the earth's foundations.
>
> I was beside him like an architect. I was his daily source of joy, always happy in his presence - happy with the world and pleased with the human race.

In this proverb it is seen that the call of wisdom is given in multiple places. God is always calling to us to receive His guidance and instructions. If such a call is answered, life would be lived meaningfully and full of purpose until we depart this world.

This chapter of Proverbs also tells us about the importance of choosing wisdom and avoiding foolishness at all cost. For wisdom to be chosen, the Bible now tells us that wisdom is calling out and reason is making herself heard on the hilltops. Wisdom appeals to all and wisdom calls everyone regardless of who they are and where they come, whether today or during the time when the Gospel message was not received. Those who hunger for this treasure of wisdom must take heed to wisdom's call by adjusting their everyday lifestyle and being obedient to the call.

Ip Tekes Piu in the legend took heed to the higher calling, re-adjusted his routine and was successful in reaching the call. After all, wisdom's call is God's call, and, according to Psalm 27:8, whoever listens carefully to this call and obeys it will enjoy life's journey till God calls them home.

Wisdom was there first even before the world began. Imagine, before God created the ocean and the spring of waters, before the mountains hills and the valleys were designed and created, before the sky was set in place with its stars, sun, moon, universe and planets, its solar system was created and the foundation of the earth was laid. Wisdom was beside the creator God as an architect sourcing Him with pure joy. Then it's not a waste of time to take heed to the call of wisdom. Ip Tekes Piu got his reward for responding to the call of the Kundu drum.

Wisdom also promises to pour out and make God's words known to us (Proverbs 1:20-23). This is the promise of planting the Word through the Holy Spirit. This promise came true when the Word was planted in the womb of Mary by the power of the Holy Spirit and she brought forward the Saviour of the world, who became flesh and blood in the world (1 John 1:1).

Furthermore, in Genesis 1:1 the Bible tells us that in the beginning, when the earth was formless with its raging ocean, the Spirit of the Lord was hovering over the waters.

This therefore tells us that, wisdom is also the Holy Spirit, according to Proverbs 8. That means the Holy Spirit who is the wisdom of God was there at the beginning.

Later when Christ came down to this world to offer salvation to mankind, He was also regarded as wisdom, according to 1 Corinthians 1:30. In other words, the biblical definition of Wisdom and Christ is one and the same.

1 Corinthians 1:24 [NLT] goes on to say,

> But to those called by God to salvation, both Jews and
> Gentiles, Christ is the Power of God and the Wisdom of God.

Since the good News about Jesus as the wisdom of God was going to be reaching this part of the tribe, God Father, God Son and God Holy Spirit begins with an open call in the streets and hilltops where everyone can see and hear. God's calling is not a secret matter but an open call that goes out to the simple, scoffers and fools, where wisdom extends an invitation.

In Legend One, the beating of the kundu drum, and it's

never-ending call that attracted all the young men of the valley, was like the call of wisdom described in Proverbs 8 and Proverbs 1:20-23.

The young man was only able to do a successful climb because he was humble and listened to his inner voice giving him direction. He also had a strong desire to reach the mountain top and investigate the call of the kundu and see for himself what this call was all about. The Bible says Wisdom is more precious than rubies (Proverbs 8:1), but one must be willing to pay like this young man to find it. And only few are willing to make such sacrifice, like this successful young man who climbed high and low and brought the owner of the melody back home. Taking special care of her, he was rewarded with the good things she offered.

It was only fitting that God planted this truth in the Legend of the Call of the Kundu Drum, an everyday household legend passed down from generation to generation. He knew that such a vital message would be received by all people of the valley through all generations.

He did this so that the simple and scoffers, like the lost tribes of the children of Mendi valley, who were only exposed to the outside world in the early 1950's, will know about the open call of Christ when the Gospel does reach them at a given time.

B. The Call To Worship

The second part of this legend now seen in the light of the Gospel was the call to worship. It is clear throughout the scriptures that God's ultimate purpose for creating humans and placing them on earth is to properly and totally worship Him. It is a call from God to bring His people into His presence. Even when Christ returns and we get to Heaven, a glimpse of how we will worship in Heaven is shown to John in Revelation chapter 4.

Worshiping God the creator is the call of the Gospel. Worship helps to refocus in order for one to worship the living God and to remember God's powerfulness, greatness and kindness. And in this legend, that's actually what's happening as the young man reaches the top of the mountain. He sees God's glory at its peak as the wonders of Nature surround him. He sees the majestic power of God at work below, above and all around him. He sat quietly with adoration and reverence paying tribute and homage to the Creator for His goodness and powerfulness. The young man's distracted heart and eyes were turned towards God and he momentarily forgot the real reason that he was there. This call can bring peace and joy everlasting.

In Romans 11:36 [GNT] the Bible says that

> For all things were created by him, and all things exist through him and for him. To God be glory forever and ever! Amen.

This means the whole Earth belongs to the Lord as He alone created it. God founding and establishing the whole earth through such a degree of creativity and design is so inspiring and comforting. It reveals His glory, passion and His great love for the earth, therefore He deserves all glory, honour and praise. We give all this back to Him in the act of worship as it's a summons from God. In the legend Tekes Piu laid himself aside as he momentarily forgot about the attractive melody of the Kundu and his reason for the difficult and dangerous journey, and recognised God in creation. He gave this unknown God the adoration, reverence and homage that He is due.

It is also evident in 1 Chronicles 16:31-34, people can worship God for His goodness and steadfast love. It also shows how all of creation throughout the world worships God. Hosea 6:6 further declares that God desires worship, intimate and special. Like the young man in this legend, worship of God should occur in all places due to His mighty deeds and powerful acts. He alone is worthy to be praised and adored.

The earth belongs to the Lord and the Lord alone, for He created it. We are expected to praise and worship the Lord God for creating the world and also creating us. This statement is on the mind of every Christian today. However, in the times of the ancestors of the people of the Mendi valley, the expectation to worship God as the Creator of the world was unknown - until the truth of the Gospel was brought in by missionaries.

Because our God is the Beginning and the Ending, and He being an Omnipotent God, He had to leave a trace of Himself, being the Creator. In the legend being discussed, the call of the Kundu was such that men left whatever they were doing and looked up to the high mountains with longing in their hearts. They all tried to find a way to reach the top to find the source of the Kundu, but all failed.

They all failed due to their own pride, but this one young man was successful because he was led by this inner voice to be humble. He took the time to listen and to obey carefully. The little rat taking him up the dangerous track is now seen as the Holy Spirit who led him to the top of the mountain, where he enjoyed the view and the breathtaking wonder of creation by an unknown, but very powerful God. He even momentarily forgot the reason for his most dangerous journey and the never-ending longing that attracted him upwards..

The God of Israel is the only one true and powerful God, who owns the whole universe (from stone aged societies to the world's top civilised nations). Despite the world's latest technology, knowledge and super powers, no one can be like Him, for everything belongs to Him and only Him. We are not worthy of Him, for nobody is worthy to be like God. He is such a Holy and powerful God. That's why in the legend, no man was able to go up to the mountain despite their attempts. No one was like Him.

The one young man who successfully climbed the mountain top is represented by the few eligible people who will go up to the mountain to worship Him. Those kinds of people are the ones who are pure in act and in thoughts, who do not worship any other Gods and make false promises (Psalms 24:3-4).

Such people will be blessed like this young man who was blessed with the breathtaking beauty of creation and the graceful woman who plays the kundu that all men long to see. He brings her home and finds great wealth inside her heart as he operates on her.

The woman represents a temple. In the temple is found the word of God and the word of God is full of Wisdom. That's what Ip Tekes Piu finds and brings home.

This particular tribe belonged to God because they were also part of His creation. God just did not decide to create the world one day, He also planned for it and designed a system of organisation so the earth works as it does from the beginning. God is so much more powerful than any other gods or beings of this world. For no one can surpass His power. Therefore, He had a plan for these children of the Mendi valley. So as a reassurance, he visited their cultures and embedded Himself in their legends, assuring them that there is a God, the Father, who is guiding them in these furthest unknown parts of the world that He owns.

God had left a nugget of truth in this Legend which was an important way of handing down information from generation to generation by telling these people that those whose lives were as worthy will go up to the mountains and be blessed with God's goodness. They will also enter the temple and find good things inside it. They will worship Him in truth and spirit as He really is, instead of their pagan worship of other gods.

Footprint Two

THE TWELVE BROTHERS

The virgin Birth and the Devil are exposed in the story of the twelve brothers. The word of God says the Devil came to steal, kill and destroy while Christ came to give life and life in full abundance.

A. The Devil came to steal, kill and to destroy

In John 10:10 [GNT], Jesus said:

The thief comes only in order to steal, kill and destroy. I have come to give life - life in all its fullness.

This destructive method of the devil mentioned in God's powerful Word is seen when the story of the old man who represents the old devil is told in the legend. This vital message was embedded in the legend long before the good news of the Gospel was spread worldwide.

In the legend of the twelve brothers, the devil is mysteriously steals and kills all eleven brothers. All twelve brothers are about to be destroyed until the virgin birth.

The fall of the devil happened already before the birth of Christ the Saviour of the world.

Revelation 12:7-9 [GNT] says:

> Then war broke out in heaven. Michael and his angels fought against the dragon, who fought back with his angels; but the dragon was defeated, and he and his angels were not allowed to stay in heaven any longer. The huge dragon was thrown out - that ancient serpent, named the Devil, or Satan, that deceived the whole world. He was thrown down to earth, and all his angels with him.

And these angels that have been thrown out of Heaven came down to steal, kill and destroy, as Jesus himself said in John 10:10. For the Devil to defeat the world through his network, the devil knows he has only a limited time, therefore he is filled with rage.

With only a short time left before he is defeated by the blood of the Lamb of God, his ways are cunning and techniques more deceptive. People are called to be alert and be watchful for,

> Your enemy, the Devil, roams around like a roaring lion looking for someone to devour.
>
> 1 Peter 5:8b [GNT]

It was important that this message was given to the children of this primitive world in their own day to day culture so that when the Good News of Salvation reached the people, they could readily accept it gladly, for it was already told over and over again in their culture. It did not become raw information that the people found hard to swallow. It was already a part of their society and system.

B. The Virgin Birth: Christ came to give life and life in full abundance

In the legend, no man slept with the woman to make her pregnant. She conceived supernaturally. This is the same story of Jesus our Lord. Mary the mother of Jesus did not have to lay down with Joseph to be pregnant; she also conceived supernaturally.

After the fall of man in the Garden of Eden in Genesis

chapter 3, the biblical record of the Old Testament foretold Christ's supernatural birth. The Lord spoke in judgement to the Devil after the seduction of Eve and the fall of Adam,

> *"...I will put enemnity between you and the woman,*
>
> *And between your seed and her seed,*
>
> *He shall bruise you on the head, And you shall bruise him on the heel."*
>
> *Genesis 3:15 [NASB]*

The reference here is to the seed of the woman, not the seed of the man. Only a unique seed and supernatural seed could accomplish that unique and supernatural victory of bruising the head of the serpent. That means, no son by an ordinary generation of Adam's ruined race could accomplish God's extraordinary plan of salvation. The adequate cause is found in the woman's seed. A virgin born Saviour is foretold in the Garden of Eden when God judges the fallen Adam, Eve and the deceiver.

It is also prophesied in the book of Isaiah 7:14 [KJV]:

> *Therefore the Lord Himself shall give you a sign; Behold, a virgin shall conceive, and bear a son, and shall call his name Immanuel.*

As first announced by God in the Garden of Eden, God in Christ has a supernatural programme to destroy the works of the devil. In the fall of Adam in Eden, the origin of enmity is found between God and the devil. Because of this enmity, sin and the devil and all his works must be destroyed, thus the declaration of the virgin birth. Only God could see that the works of the devil will be destroyed.

The birth of the Saviour is further announced in the New Testament:

> *This is how the birth of Jesus Christ took place. His mother Mary was engaged to Joseph, but before they were married, she found out that she was going to have a baby by the Holy Spirit. Joseph was a man who always did what was right, but he did not want to disgrace Mary publicly; so he made plans to break the engagement privately. While he was thinking*

> about this, an angel of the Lord appeared to him in a dream and said, "Joseph, descendant of David, do not be afraid to take Mary to be your wife. For it is by the Holy Spirit that she has conceived. She will have a son and you will name him Jesus - because he will save his people from their sins".
>
> Now all this happened in order to make come true what the Lord had said through the prophet, "A virgin will become pregnant and have a son, and he will be called Immanuel" (which means, "God is with us").
>
> So when Joseph woke up, he married Mary, as the angel of the Lord had told him to. But he had no sexual relations with her before she gave birth to her son. And Joseph named him Jesus.
>
> Matthew 1:18-24 [GNT]

It was going to be a virgin who was going to conceive to have the promised Immanuel.

> For there is one God and one mediator between God and mankind, the man Jesus Christ.
>
> 1 Timothy 2:5 [NIV]

Apart from the virgin birth we would have no mediator.

Because people have fallen short of the Glory of God due to their own sinfulness, a unique Saviour with a unique birth was going to appear. A unique Saviour to bridge the gap between man and God was to be born, and that good news will reach the children of Mendi Valley in the near future. The good news of Salvation from Jesus who came to destroy the works of the Devil was going to be the most important news of all times.

After the fall of Eve and Adam in the Garden of Eden, sin had come into the world. No one is pure in thoughts, actions or words. All have sinned and fallen short of the Glory of God. In the eyes of God all men were lost in their own wickedness. The Lost brothers in the legend represented the lostness of mankind in their sinfulness.

The young boy turning himself to a mosquito and entering the womb of the virgin represents the birth of Jesus Christ through the Virgin Mary.

The Son of Man came to seek and to save the lost.

Luke 19:10 [GNT]

The old father of the girls represents the old serpent. That's why he was using his fallen angels to steal and kill the brothers. That's the ultimate plan the devil has for every human on Earth. He lures away people with his lies and cunning ways and destroys them.

Despite Lucifer's destructive character, he has been a looser and will always be a looser, for the seed of Eve will crush the head of the serpent. Thus, God's salvation plan was through the virgin birth of the Saviour Jesus Christ, the Son of God. The boy born of the virgin woman in the legend was able to face the old devil and kill him, just like Christ Jesus who won victory over the Devil will kill him.

The Saviour was the only one who was able to gather the lost sheep and rescue them from death. This was told in the story of the the virgin birth, the one who killed the devil after studying all his techniques and brought the brothers back to life, just like Christ who rescues the world from deadly sins.

Brave missionaries who will be called by God will bring the Good News, but God in His mercy had prepared the hearts of the people to pave the way for the gospel. God had already embedded the story of the lost sinners, the fallen angels, the virgin birth and Christ's saving Grace in their very own cultures. This is the legend of the twelve brothers which has been told, retold and handed down from generations over and over again.

God is so powerful and merciful. He was able to teach the salvation plan to the natives of a faraway land even before the Good News was preached across the world. Truely God's ways are not our ways and His thoughts are not like our thoughts. He was able to set the person of Jesus within the context of Mendi oral traditions. Powerful and mysterious are His ways.

Footprint Three

POREAH HINN & KOLUM

*I*n this legend, offerings, sacrifices, obligation and reciprocation, give and take, become the focus of the discussion in the light of the gospel of Jesus Christ.

Offerings and Sacrifices

The Old Testament rules and regulations have many complicated details and the overall sacrificial system may be quite foreign to this strange far-away land of Papua New Guinea. Even then, one could hardly underestimate the significance of the Old Testament sacrificial system of the chosen people of God, the Jews. It was an order outlined and given by the Almighty God of Israel. It was meant to be followed.

Offerings and sacrifices were a vital part of the practice of a standing relationship with God in the times of Cain and Abel to Noah and Moses. After that, the direction came from God through His servant Moses to build the tabernacle, the design of which was given by God Himself. Offerings and sacrifices continued to remain as a central part of the worship system of the tabernacle and the first and second temples, before destruction by Babylon due to Israel turning to foreign gods and disobeying their one true God.

The Bible says God commanded Moses to make an altar for Him.

> Make an altar of earth for me, and on it sacrifice your sheep and your cattle as offerings to be completely burned and as fellowship offerings. In every place that I set aside for you to worship me, I will come to you and bless you.
>
> Exodus 20:24 [GNT]

According to the earthen altar law in the text above, and the many other references to such altars in the early history of Israel as a nation in Canaan the Promised Land, the God of Israel wanted the Israelites to be worshipping at them despite the existance of the tabernacle altar. These altars and the worship practices were relatively simple compared to the altars and worship system in the sanctuary, that is the tabernacle and later the temple.

The Bible continues to teach in Genesis concerning offering and sacrifices:

> After some time Cain brought some of his harvest and gave it as an offering to the LORD. Then Abel brought the first lamb born to one of his sheep, killed it, and gave the best part of it as an offering. The LORD was pleased with Abel and his offering.
>
> Genesis 4: 3-4 [GNT]

Even as early as the beginning of the world, the above Scripture informs us that sacrifices and offerings were a crucial part of the worship of God that existed. Cain brought an offering to the Lord from the fruit of the ground while Abel brought one from his flock.

To give a few more examples of Scriptures with references to sacrifices, Noah also build an altar in Genesis 8:20, while Jacob offered a sacrifice in the hill country in Genesis 46:1.

Finally, the Bible says,

> [Moses] got up early the next morning and built an altar at the foot of the mountain... Then he sent young Israelite men, and they offered burnt offerings and sacrificed young bulls as fellowship offerings to the Lord.
>
> Exodus 24:4-5 [NIV]

Despite the existence of the tabernacle, the chosen nation of God continued to offer burnt, grain, drink and peace offerings on earthen altars as well as tabernacle altars. In fact, the Lord commanded them to build such an altar at Mt.Ebal where burnt and peace offerings would be sacrificed.

Therefore, all references to offerings and sacrifices above show that this system was a central part of worshipping the God of Israel. It was so important that such sacrifices and offerings were practiced for a very long time in those days. God allowed it as it was indeed pleasing to Him.

In His very powerful ways, God gave prior witness of His existence and the importance of sacrifice and offering systems by embedding them in the cultures of the children of a faraway land, who would become His children through the offering and sacrifice of His son Jesus Christ. He did that through the legend of *Poreah Hinn Kolum*.

The two men lived their own lives without the understanding of a higher authority, but the Mountain god called them to give offerings and sacrifices from the produce of their lands as well as animals they have raised. Then, as they harvested produce from their land, they came to the realisation that there was a higher god who expected something to be given back to him. With the two men living in obedience to this expectation from a higher authority, their very own need was met by that god. They were blessed with two beautiful woman and their bride prices. When we live in obedience to the word of God, He blesses us with what we need for the present time. That's what He did for the two brothers.

Blessings Resulting from Offerings and Sacrifices

In Exodus 20:24, discussed above, God calls Moses to build the altar of earth and worship Him there. God Himself will come down and bless him at the altar of sacrifice and worship.

Offerings and sacrifices are beneficial for the person who is engaged in this activity. Sacrifices and offerings seem to be the key that unlocks the doors to people's deliverance and blessings. The returns of sacrifices are reaped bountifully in joy as the returns are beyond what can be explained by human words. It's God's ordained way to a new beginning, glorious living and a series of breakthroughs in this world.

The word of God discusses some benefits to sacrifices and offerings. For example; Genesis 1:21 talks about the reversal of curses, or 2 Samuel 24:22-25 where termination of plagues are discussed, or the altar of supernatural turnaround in 1 Kings 17:8-16. Curses are reversed and plagues were terminated because the children of Israel were living in obedience to their God when it came to sacrifices and offerings.

In the legend, when the two brothers learnt of the god who lives in the forest on the mountain and his request of sacrifices and offerings from their produce and of their animals, they offered willingly and in obedience.

God enacted a covenant of blessings, multiplication and dominion with Abraham and his descendants because of Abraham's obedient and faithful walk with his God. This was also the case for the two brothers; they offered their sacrifices without questions or doubts. They were then blessed with ladies and wealth beyond what they could have done for themselves. It was literally a supernatural turn around in their situations all because of their sacrifices and offerings in faith to an unseen God.

Giving always results in receiving. We have God's word on it. Give to others and God will give to you. Indeed you will receive a full measure, a generous helping poured into your hands, all you can hold, (Luke 6:38). When the two brothers in the legend became givers as required by the god who lived in a nearby mountain, they automatically moved themselves into the realm of a receiver. God paid them back for their commitment and they became the founding fathers of that land as they reproduced with those wives provided to them by the god they sacrificed to regularly.

God planted this seed of truth of offerings, sacrifices and its advantages in the legend. He did this because He was going to sacrifice His best by giving His Son who knew no sin, to reconcile the world to Himself. This soon coming event had to be announced to the most remote and far away land in the world in their own day to day culture. God truly is powerful and His mercies truly never come to an end.

Footprint Four

THE CHEATING CUSCUS

The cheating cuscus was the story of Eve and Adam in the Garden of Eden. The relationship between Eve and Adam was at its best in the perfect garden planted by God Himself. They lived happily until the serpent comes into the picture and becomes a major player in the drama of the garden.

It seems clear from the word of God that, there was an actual walking serpent in this perfect garden, described as one of the animals God has created (Genesis 1:25; 2:19). The serpent definitely wasn't a supernatural being, satan only borrowed the body of the serpent to tempt Eve. The serpent was the instrument the devil used to do his bidding, therefore, the tempter was the devil that was disguised in the form of a snake. The snake plays the role of a trickster like the cuscus in this legend. Snakes are not common around this area, so the cuscus was used as the deceiver, as the people in this part of the land were familiar with this creature.

Satan borrowed and used the body of the snake in the Garden of Eden. Similarly the cuscus in the legend borrows the body of the brother of the girl and plays dirty tricks in their garden as well. The cheating cuscus and satan also play the same role. Satan entered the serpent, a real creature, to purposely deceive Eve. The craftiness of the devil is now found in this legend when the cuscus borrowed the skin of the hunter to bring destruction to his innocent sister, who was unaware of such craftiness by the devil. By the time the hunter brother arrives, he faces the destruction created by the tricking, lying and destructive devil, by entering the cuscus like he entered the serpent in the Garden of Eden.

Satan was cast out of Heaven and out of God's presence because of his rebellion against God. The Bible calls him the 'god of this age' and 'the prince of the power of the air'. In John 8:44, the devil is also called the 'father of all lies'. There is no single truth in him. His main function is to deceive, lie and bring destruction to the lives of people mercilessly. This deception will continue until his future judgement, when Christ will end his inglorious career one final day.

With the fall of the devil, his wisdom and intellect is being used for evil craftiness. Eve and Adam, who had dominion over all creatures, were being tempted by the same devil working through an inferior being. After all, Eve and Adam were vulnerable to temptation as they were oblivious to evil, not knowing where the traps lay, whereas satan did and used his craftiness to take advantage of Eve and Adam's integrity.

Satan's policy has been to deceive, ever since the Garden of Eden, where his deceptive technique led to the great fall of humans (Genesis 3:1). After the fall, Eve and Adam were thrown out of the Garden of Eden. So are the brother and sister in this legend. They were also thrown out of the comfort, safety and security of their own home due to the deception of the cheating cuscus.

After his fall, the devil became the god or prince of this world. This defeated foe continues to be a traitor, liar and deceiver for that's his nature (Job 8:44). Deception has always been one of the most powerful weapons that the Devil, who is also known as the serpent, the great dragon, Beelzebub and the kingdom of darkness possesses, used continually against God's own people (Isaiah 44:20). He 'roams around like a roaring lion' seeking to destroy or deceive and use whoever makes himself available (1Peter 5:8).

After the fall God also had a great plan, that's why upon pronouncing Judgement,

> The LORD God said to the serpant...
> "...I will put enemnity Between you and the woman,
> And between your seed and her seed,
> He shall bruise you on the head,
> And you shall bruise him on the heel."
>
> *Genesis 3:15 [NASB]*

While pronouncing judgement, the Father of the universe also announced His great plan of salvation. Through a woman who did not lie with a man, a Saviour was going to be born. This Saviour was going to crush the head of the serpent the deceiver. Jesus Christ came down later through a virgin birth and fulfilled this very scripture. By His blood He bought us back to Himself, and by His powerful resurrection he crushed the head of the serpent devil, who is now a defeated foe.

The cheating techniques and the great salvation plan were told over and over again in the form of the legend of the cheating cuscus in a faraway land where the gospel in God's grace would reach in a very long time.

This is because,

> God loved the world so much that he gave his only one Son, so that everyone who bellieves in him may not die but have eternal life.
>
> *John 3:16 [GNT]*

His love goes beyond the Jews and reaches the Gentiles of the tribal nations.

His love was unconditional and this is taught in Romans 8:38-39 [NASB]:

> *For I am convinced that neither death, nor life, nor angels, nor principalities, nor things present, nor things to come, nor powers, nor height, nor depth, nor any other created thing, shall be able to separate us from the love of God, which is in Christ Jesus our Lord.*

Footprint Five

THE TALKING TARO

*I*n this legend, Jesus Christ as the House of Bread and Bread of Life was told and retold. Moreover, this legend of the stolen talking Taro also tells the story of Ruth and Naomi.

To discuss Jesus Christ as the House of Bread, the two women in this legend represent the Gentile people. The Taro represents the word of God, as bread was not known at that time in this part of the valley.

It is stolen because they are not Israelites. They represent the Gentile people who do not belong to the House of Bread. God's plan for the nation of Israel is not only for the Messiah, the glory of His people Israel, but also a light to lighten the darkness in the Gentile nations far and near.

The Old Testament frequently mentions that God's plan encompasses not only Jews but Gentile nations as well. In the book of Isaiah for example, Isaiah prophesied that the Gentiles would come to the light.

> *He says, "It is a small thing that You should be My Servant*
>
> *To raise up the tribes of Jacob and to restore the preserved ones of Israel;*

> *I will also make You a light of the nations*
> *So that My salvation may reach to the ends of the earth."*
>
> Isaiah 49:6 [NASB]

The New Testament also confirms God's salvation plan for the Gentiles as well. Mathew 12:21 [NASB] for instance:

> *... in His Name the Gentiles will hope.*

1 Corinthians 1:24 [GNT] also says:

> *but for those whom God has called, both Jews and Gentiles, this message is Christ, who is the power of God and wisdom of God.*

Ephesians 2:14 [GNT] continues the theme to say:

> *For Christ himself has brought us peace by making Jews and Gentiles one people. With His own body he broke down the wall that separated them and kept them enemies.*

God had important plans for Gentile people from this part of the land. Therefore, in His greatness He also embedded this great plan in their very own cultural Legend of the Talking Taro.

To give a brief description of this root plant called Taro, it is a starchy root vegetable cultivated in Asia and the Pacific Islands but now enjoyed around the world. It has a brown outer skin and white flesh. When cooked it has a mildly sweet taste and is a great source of fibre. It's also full of flavour when cooked on an open fire.

The aroma of a freshly cooked taro over an open fire and hot ashes is clean, clear and refreshing. The smell itself is warm and mouth-watering. When freshly removed out of hot ashes, it imparts a roasted cracker-like flavour and the air is so thick with aroma, just like baked bread out of an oven. Taro was an important food in this part of the land during the Stone Age period. It was called men's food. When harvest time came people would gather, for the gardener would share the taro among relatives from far and near, and also repay those who have shared with him during their harvest.

1. Jesus the House of Bread

Bethlehem, which means 'house of bread', is first mentioned in Genesis 35:19. This would mean a place where one could come and eat when hungry, as food supply could be found there always. There is nothing you can't find in Bethlehem.

Bethlehem becomes a place of hope for the one who weeps in Jeremiah 31:15-17. In the story of Ruth and Naomi, a place of blessing after all they lost. They are blessed with a kinsman-Redeemer through whom Ruth becomes the great grandmother to King David, in the line of Jesus, the Bread of Life.

Not only can they find bread when hungry or blessings in their desperation, but in Bethlehem kings are anointed, for instance, King David in 1 Samuel 16:1-3, or Jesus the Son of God is also born in the place that means the house of bread (Matthew 1:1).

Bethlehem, the House of Bread, is also the place of salvation as the place brings forward the birth of the Saviour of the world. Therefore, this message needed to be told in the cultures of such far away lands, so God in His wisdom installed the story of the House of Bread in the talking taro - a special crop which looks, smells and tastes like bread when cooked in hot ashes.

It's no coincidence that a taro was used instead of bread in the legend, as bread was never heard of in this faraway land at that time. The one food that could resemble Bread when baked was Taro, especially when roasted over an open fire and cooked in the hot ashes. It smells and taste just like bread when freshly baked. That's why taro is being used in this legend.

It also is not a mistake that Jesus was born in a small place called Bethlehem, the House of Bread, for that was actually what the body of Christ was all about. Being born in the House of Bread, His body is now the Bread of Life.

In the Scripture in John 6:35 [GNT], Jesus says:

> *"I am the bread of life,"* Jesus told them. *"Those who come to me will never be hungry..."*

In the legend, the two women in their hunger would walk to this particular house where it was warm and welcoming. The fireplace always had a taro cooking and they would steal from it. After satisfying their hunger, they would get a piece of burning wood and walk back home to make their own fire.

Jesus becomes the bread, food and life, as stated through the Bible. He becomes the daily mana for the children of Israel in the desert. He also becomes the showbread in the Jerusalem temple built by King Solomon. He is also the one who becomes the sustainer of the widow and his son through the prophet Elijah.

In the New Testament, he is the Bread of Life that's feeding the 5,000 people with just five loaves of bread. He is the Lord of the final meal on Earth with His disciples called the Lord's Supper.

Jesus therefore was transformed into Bread of Heaven throughout His life here on Earth.

After the Bread of Life was broken, died and yet rose again, Christ Jesus was ready to give Life in Heaven, the real House of Bread.

The two women did not know the owner of the house but they did not stop stealing either. The sweet taste of the taro was irresistible and the supply never ran out. When the owner of the house one day came looking for what belonged to Him, they were dumbfounded for this man was like no other man they have ever seen or heard of. Every step he took, the earth shock, and his voice had an extraordinary ring in it. His eyes looked right through their souls. They were speechless. After all, they did not know the owner of the taros in the house of taro. They sat trembling for all they did, lying exposed before this all knowing and all understanding man.

Legends of the Mendi Valley

Taro baked in hot ashes

The already consumed taro could no longer remain silent within their stomachs. They could feel its voice responding from right within. The Taro had become alive and was talking in the depth of their tummies as they heard the owner's voice. The Taro was now responding to the Creator. Of course, the bread from the House of Bread was alive and active.

> *For the word of God is alive and active. Sharper than any double-edged sword, it penetrates even to dividing soul and spirit, joints and marrow; it judges the thoughts and attitudes of the heart.*
>
> *Hebrews 4:12 [NIV]*

The Word of God is living and active and the word that was made flesh was Jesus Himself. It was part of the grace of God for the eternal security of the true Christian, whether Jews or Gentiles, not to fall away but to be saved by the Grace of God through his son Jesus, the word who has become flesh.

2. Ruth and Naomi

There is also a trace of Ruth and Naomi in the Legend of the Talking Taro. The beautiful story of Ruth and Naomi is told in the book of Ruth in the Old Testament. The name Ruth means 'grace' and the story of Ruth and Naomi demonstrates God's grace towards both the Jews and the Gentiles. Ruth, despite her status of being a Moabite (Gentile) woman, received blessings from God that she did not merit.

The story of Ruth in fact is a beautiful example of God's loving Grace. The Moabites were loathed by the Hebrews because they were pagan worshippers and worshipped the false god Chemosh. However, God in His grace selected Ruth to be a direct ancestor of the most powerful King, Jesus Christ. Ruth ended up in such an important position in the family lineage of Jesus Christ because she was full of kindness, selfless love, compassion and a 'not giving up so easily' type of attitude which she had towards her widow stepmother, Naomi, as found in Ruth 1:16-17 [NIV]:

> *Where you go I will go, and where you stay I will stay. Your people will be my people and your God [will be] my God. Where you die I will die, and there I will be buried.*

Once in Bethlehem, Ruth sustained herself and her mother-in-law by gleaning kernels from the barley harvest. One day, she meets the owner of the barley field, Boaz ,who receives her kindly and becomes her kinsman-redeemer.

This book of Ruth points us to Jesus the ultimate kinsmen-redeemer before he was even born. Ruth is the story of a young Moabite woman who came to the Love of God and the joy of belonging to His people through her Jewish mother in-law, Naomi.

Boaz was a man who had concern for others by loving his neighbours as himself. As owner of a field, Boaz showed generosity and compassion to the less fortunate. Boaz's kinsman-redemption in Ruth 4:7-10 points us to Jesus.

In the legend of the talking Taro, the older woman kept sending the younger girl to the owner of the House of

Taro. She would obediently go there and steal taro from the owner's cooking place. This went on for a while until the owner caught them by surprise in their own house, and marries the girl. They then lived happily after.

In the story of Ruth and Naomi, Ruth was sent to the barley fields by her mother-in-law so she would bring something for them to sustain their lives with, until Boaz finds her and becomes her kinsman-redeemer. While in the legend of the talking Taro, the same thing is happening; the mother keeps sending her daughter to the house of taro until the owner finds out and marries her.

Every legend at their core contains a seed of truth, unlike myths. For these two stories from two separate worlds to be so similar, only God could have planted them into the culture of these pagan Mendi people. After all, the people in this part of the land were like the Moabite people, so they needed to know this good news of a kinsman-redeemer that points directly to the work of salvation that Jesus would do for us all on the cross of Calvary, for both the Jews and the Gentile.

Footprint Six

THE EVIL GRANDMOTHER

This Legend also portrays the devil and his clever techniques using his destructive weapons in his ultimate purpose to destroy the world. The legend points to three different main points in the light of the gospel. The Devil's Destructive Plan, working out the Devil's Technique, and Light in the Dark.

1. The Devil's Destructive Plan

The Bible warns us to be watchful at all time. For example, 1 Peter 5:8-10 [GNT]:

> Be alert, be on watch! Your enemy, the Devil, roams around like a roaring lion, looking for someone to devour. Be firm in your faith and resist him, because you know that other believers in all the world are going through the same kind of sufferings.

To withstand the roar of satan and to fear no more, this was the message from Peter to the believers in the first century, as Christians became hard targets for the devil and his followers. Targeting the followers of Christ started at the birth of Jesus, when Herod captured and slaughtered all the boys supposed to be a similar age as the boy Jesus.

Then Jesus was met head on by the devil in the wilderness and came under attack. Even the Sanhedrin attacked him until His death on the cross and His burial. However, His burial was not the end of the story. His powerful resurrection was the hope for all Christians. Yet evil continued to target the apostles even as they preached - all except John were targeted to die by forces of evil. Despite all this, the word of God has been preached, recorded and preserved for time and eternity. Therefore, victory is assured for all God's people, for we have the word which is the power of God unto victory.

Even so people have to be on alert still, for the devil roams around like a roaring lion to devour anybody weak in faith.

This warning was told in the legend of the war with the evil grandmother. The devil in this legend is using her deceptive techniques again to deceive the innocent brother and sister, to devour them. If the young boy gave vent to fear and doubts, then they would have been defeated. However, he stood his grounds and won victory. It's a story of faith, strength, and courage.

God calls us to live under His shadow so that we find safety and divine protection in Him, for He who is in us is greater than he who is in the world. No matter who is against you, if we declare the almighty God as our defender, He will always protect us (Psalm 91).

The boy wrestles for a few days and one whole night with the evil grandmother, who was totally bent on devouring the both of them. We must never forget that there is a very spiritual side to battle in the world, as the Scripture in Ephesians 6:12 says that we wrestle with principalities and powers, with the rulers of the darkness of this world, and with spiritual wickedness in higher places.

The devil is real because the Bible says so. The devil's destructive actions are also real as this world is full of war, disunity and deep hatred brought on by other human beings like Hitler, and others causing destruction motivated by evil. And at a very personal level, the trials and temptations brought to us every day also tell of the reality of the existence of the devil, satan.

When the devil and his angels were thrown out of heaven, God knew they would be on earth bringing destruction at all levels.

Therefore, in this legend, it seems that God was preparing this side of the world for the Gospel already even before Christ did come to the world. As such, the people were able to accept the gospel soon enough, for God had planted awareness of the destructive behaviour of the devil in their very own culture and legends. The message of the gospel was not so new to them. It was a story handed down from generation to generation and told and retold over and over again.

2. Working out the Devil's Techniques

Satan is a real working spirit that people hear and see in the world around them. With his power he can tempt people and lead them astray. As Christians we struggle against temptation and trials directed at us from the forces of wickedness in the heavenly places (Ephesians 6:12). Yes, the roar of a lion is scary but we should not be overcome or be scared of the spiritual battles in which we are engaged. Like the boy in the legend, who confidently planned his attack strategy against the wicked old woman and won his battle.

The people in the valley did have a powerful enemy of their soul. They needed to know something about that enemy to make it through. Just like in a war, one needs to know the characteristics of the enemy. Only in that way, can people have a strategy for fighting and staying alive.

For example, in the Legend of the Evil Grandmother, the young girl did not recognise the enemy, resulting in her taking sides with the enemy, which almost brought destruction to the both of them. However, the young man knew what he was dealing with, resulting in him developing strategies to help in his war with the evil grandmother. Despite the evil grandmother's determination to devour the two of them, knowing something about the enemy and keeping helpful strategies in place helped the young man to save both of them from being completely devoured.

Just beyond our vision, the predator is there, stalking us and looking for signs of weakness. He is ready to pounce and devour mercilessly and without compassion, making us his prey. Having our defence strategies in place and standing strong in our faith in Jesus Christ will be the only way to escape from the grip of the devil.

Just like the evil grandmother in the legend, the devil hangs loose around the place, hunting to devour people weak in the faith. As a protective pathway in dealing with the devil, God, through Peter, gives us the design for resisting the devil in all his manifestations.

Peter calls us to be sober, to be aware of the devil's deceptive lie. Sober-minded is to be calm and collected, with good sense and judgment in wisdom. Then our thoughts can be shielded from the devil's ridiculous and crazy thoughts that try to grab our mind. Instead, grab hold of God's word and His Holy Spirit. That's actually how the boy in the legend acted. He was so sober-minded and alert that the old woman had no gap to destroy them, both he and his sister.

Learning a few lessons from the young boy in the legend, we can see that he was alert and watchful. He was wise enough to be aware of the devil's technique and his deceptive, destructive plans and was able to defeat this roaring lion by standing his ground firmly. His consistency in his approach in the battle helped him win his battle all the way through.

Every warfare is based on deception. If you know the enemy and also know who you are and where you stand in terms of facing the enemy, you will not need to fear the results of the battle you are in. After all, God was establishing a strategy in this culture to make his identity known and ordaining the mindset of the people of this valley to prepare them for the gospel.

However, if you know yourself but not the enemy, defeat is on the way. Therefore in the battle with the devil, know yourself, know God and know the enemy, for you will defeat Satan as he is already a defeated foe. That's definitely what the boy in the legend did; he knew the enemy with its deceptive methods, and fought the battle over and over again until he won the victory.

3. Light in the Dark

The young man in the legend defeated evil by keeping the light going on in the dark. The devil loves the darkness because the light exposes who he is and his evil deceptive methods. An entire network of spiritual darkness spearheaded by satan himself and carried out by demonic systems silently works to influence the whole wide world. This darkness included those living in this part of the world where the legend was told. God said in Genesis 1, let there be light and there was light. This light exposes all manner of things disordered in the dark, but the light designed them in order.

This legend was, therefore, pointing to the Saviour who would come and bring the light to chase the darkness away. Jesus is known as the light of the world in John 8:12. Only through Him can people find the hope of light in the darkness. Jesus came so that the world would come out of its darkness and have light by experiencing the power of the Holy Spirit. God's loving grace through the power of His Word shed His light in a world in total darkness.

The young man represents Jesus in this legend. Jesus was the only light of heaven that was able to know the techniques of the deceiving liar called satan, and defeat him. That's why by keeping the fire alight all through the darkness, the boy was able to overcome the evil grandmother (who represented satan in this legend). Jesus brought light into the darkness that covered the world with the deception of the works of the devil.

In the legend, the young girl was deceived by the devil in order to divert her attention to the lies being told by the evil grandmother. The young girl represents people of this dark world who listen to the devil's lies and let themselves be seduced so easily by the things of this world. Because light affects everything it touches and reveals the truth where needed, the young girl learns the truth that the light was revealing everything in the total darkness. This light represents the light of Heaven. Jesus Christ was that light of hope.

Jesus is the light of the world for He is the Son of God. Apart from Jesus, people live in total darkness. However, those who follow Jesus will never live in darkness but will have the light of love. Only Jesus can bring light to the dark part of our lives. The Light of Christ is God's grace in a world made so dark by sin. Only Christ can brighten dark parts of our life, as He exposes things in the dark and sheds light in our lives. The death of Christ on the cross broke the chain of darkness, lighting the way for us.

In the beginning, in Genesis 1:4, God said, "let there be light, and there was light". He saw the light was good and He separated the light from the darkness. Jesus is the light of the world and those who do not walk in His Word are separated from Him, therefore living in the darkness. Only in Christ do we have the absolute fullness of light. And so everything the light touches, it's the very presence of Christ and His loving grace. Satan can't do much regarding the light of heaven and can't get anywhere near the light for this light only exposes him.

Finally, in this Legend of the Evil Grandmother, God has planted a seed of truth regarding the devil that roams around like a roaring lion looking out to devour anyone who is weak. He is also pointing this out to the Gentile people who live in tribes, of a Saviour who will be called the light of the world, and a Saviour to the Gentiles as well, for in the name of Jesus the Gentiles will have hope. This was a world prepared for the Gospel by God Himself.

For God says,

> *"It is a small thing that You should be My Servant*
>
> *To raise up the tribes of Jacob and to restore the preserved ones of Israel;*
>
> *I will also make You a light of the nations*
>
> *So that My salvation may reach to the ends of the earth."*
>
> *Isaiah 49:6 [NASB]*

Footprint Seven

THE TWO BROTHERS

The legend of the two brothers is linked to the story of Cain and Abel. It was told over and over again and handed down from generation to generation by the people of this land. There is also something about connection with God through Nature in this legend as well.

God wanted the people of this valley to know the Bible story of the two sons of Eve and Adam so he planted the story in the Legend of Huwai and Wapon. He also wanted them to know that God was the creator of the universe and their offering would only be accepted if there was a connection to nature, like Wapon's mountain top experiences. For God was the one who designed Nature and the whole world around us as it is now.

1. Cain and Abel

The lives of these two brothers points to the story of Cain and Abel. The legend teaches the local people some important lessons about themselves and their spiritual lives. In Genesis chapter 3 we find that human disobedience first occurred in the Garden of Eden, when Eve gives in to the deceptive lies of the serpent. That was the root of sin. God said don't eat of the tree of the knowledge of good and evil, but the serpent talked Eve into eating from the tree, an act of disobedience.

In the Legend, one brother manages to learn the proper and acceptable way of sacrificing to his best friend the Dog, and how to worship an unknown maker of the universe before the act of sacrifice. The other brother, just like Cain, becomes jealous over something he can't do well for himself, despite the opportunity laid before him.

Genesis chapter 4:1-15 records the story of Cain and Abel. In the story, Cain was a farmer while Abel becomes a shepherd. When they brought their offering, Abel's was accepted while Cain's offer was rejected. Out of jealousy, Cain got furious with Abel and killed him, which resulted in Cain being cursed by God.

In the Legend of the two brothers, the same thing happens. The other brother is not content with being a farmer. He is not satisfied with his brother bringing his blessings for both of them to enjoy. With an evil motive and evil intentions, he went to do the sacrifice. He did not even do the sacrifices in the proper order as was explained to him, disobeying his brother's instructions. Thus, his offering was unaccepted and dishonoured. Consequently, he brings destruction upon their peaceful lives.

God is seen bringing clear and prior witness of His existence through the culture of a pagan people of a tribal nation. A time was coming when they will receive the good news, that they have a Creator who will want them to obey His word and bring in acceptable offerings and sacrifices, like what Abel did. When God forbade Cain to get angry, he did not listen to God and started to get jealous and got angrier with his brother. This envy and jealousy resulted in the murder of Abel.

The two brother's story in this legend is a repetition of Cain and Abel's story in the beginning. Huwai represents Cain, who murders his brother due to faults of his own.

Both brothers made sacrifices, but Abel's was accepted just like Wapon in the legend.

Cain murders his brother, just like Huwai murders his. As a result, Cain was cursed and marked for life. The earth was now cursed with Abel's blood, therefore Cain was no longer able to farm the land. Cain is punished and becomes a fugitive and wanderer. The same sentence is applied to Huwai when he murders Wapon in the legend of the two brothers.

To conclude, in the Mendi valley, when a brother kills his own brother, the land is no longer farmable for that murderer. He and his family, especially the sons, have been cursed and they leave their customary land. A powerful teaching exists that if they eat from that land, they will surely die. Even today, no murderer of his brother tills their family land. Instead, they become a wanderer.

God had already paved the way of the Gospel in this valley even before the good news reached the land. Such was like a foundation for the declaration of Christian faith in the area.

2. Nature Testifying to God's existence.

The natural world displays the glory of God and so it's the first way to know of the Creator of the universe. Long before there was a tabernacle or temples and churches, the experience of knowing God was outdoors. The burning bush for example, when Moses was commissioned by God to lead his people out of Egypt. Or even during the times of Jesus, he was known for connecting himself to nature, like the times he would go to the wilderness for prayer, sit in silence beside the lakes, or go to the mountains or gardens to pray alone.

In the legend, Wapon sat quietly on the mountain top day by day, and God revealed Himself to him through the wonder and beauty of natural creation. Something inside his soul came alive when he was surrounded by God's splendour in nature on the mountain. God's invisible attributes were clearly seen and understood by Wapon in the legend. For the Bible says in Psalms 19:1-6 that "the sky reveals God's glory". In fact, it's a sign to the world that God does exist.

Humans are constantly reminded of His existence day and night as a silent and continual testimony for the entire human race. Wapun, the pagan worshiper in the legend, was not an exception. His awareness of God's existence was getting stronger and stronger due to the testimony in creation. This led him to seek to discover who the Creator was. When he did discover the one true God, the Creator of the whole universe, he started bringing in acceptable sacrifices. His heart was convicted by the silent and constant revelation of God's majestic power in the natural surroundings. For Wapon, he had discovered the wisdom and power of God. From the simple life form to the most complex, the living God has revealed himself to human kind like Wapon.

Because Wapon spent quality time in and around creation, he was able to recognise that Someone bigger was in control. He was able to know Nature reflected God's supernatural strength, creativity and glory. The Bible proclaims that nature gives clear testimony to God's existence.

Psalm 65:6-13 [NLT] for instance,

You formed the mountains by your power and armed youself with mighty strength.

You quieted the raging oceans with their pounding waves and silenced the shouting of the nations.

Those who live at the end of the earth stand in awe of your wonders.

From where the sun rises to whee it sets, you inspire shouts of joy.

This is actually what is happening to Wapon. From where he stands at the far ends of the world, he finds pure joy in the rivers, fields, mountains and all the beauty of creation. He truly worships the Creator before even knowing who this creator was.

The Bible continues to tell us in Romans 1:20 [NLT]:

Forever ever since the world was created, people have seen the earth and sky. Through everything God made, they can clearly see His invisible qualities - His eternal power and divine nature. So, they have no excuses for not knowing God.

Even in the Old Testament, Job speaks about God's hand in creation:

But ask the animals, and they will teach you, the birds in the sky, and they will tell you; or speak to the earth, and it will teach you, or let the fish in the sea inform you.

*Which of all these does not know that the hand of the L*ORD *has done this?*

In His hand is the life of every creature and the breath of all mankind.

Job 12:7-10 [NIV]

Prior to the arrival of Christian missionaries, God was making Himself known. All through the Bible we continue to read how the Lord communicates to his people through the skies, moon, stars, milky way or the galaxies, mountains, breeze rustling through the leaves of trees, endless green valleys, rolling hills and even small animals and their very existence.

This is indeed declared in Psalm 8:1,3 [NLT]:

*O L*ORD*, our Lord, your majestic name fills the earth!*

Your glory is higher than the heavens.

When I look at the night sky and see the work of your fingers -

the moon and the stars you set in place -

what are mere mortals that you should think about them,

human beings that you should care for them?

Nobody would care about mere humans who are not even from His chosen tribe, or so civilised and sophisticated like the Western Tribes, just some lost people living in tribal Nations in the furthest corner of the earth. But God did. Truly God is at work in the world providing evidence of Himself to people of the most remote areas with even the most twisted and corrupt cultures. Isn't our God truly wonderful, full of Mercies, Kindness and Love?

The revelation of God's word through His creation is also testified in Psalm 19:1-6 [NIV]:

> The heavens declare the glory of God;
> the skies proclaim the work of His hands.
> Day after day they pour forth speech;
> night after night they reveal knowledge.
> They have no speecho, they use no words;
> no sound is heard from them.
> Yet their voice goes out into all the earth,
> their words to the ends of the world.
> In the heavens God has pitched a tent for the sun.
> It is like a bridegroom coming out of his chamber,
> like a champion rejoicing to run his course.
> It rises at the end of the heavens and makes its circuit to the other;
> nothing is deprived of its warmth.

In the legend, Wapon was getting connected to God the Creator of the universe through nature. The truth about God was displayed right there for him to see, the sun rising and setting, the beauty of the mountains and valleys, graceful rivers, trees in the forest, immovable rocks, all gave constant testimony for him to see. And he was joyful and peaceful and gave acceptable offerings to Nature because his heart was right after connecting with the creator through nature, by seeing its beauty and the splendour of his glory. As a result of noticing nature, he noticed God more. The testimonies about God's existence from creation led Wapon to seek and to discover who God was.

God was clearly revealed in creation and Wapon in the legend became deeply aware of Him, that is why he was led by the barking dog to offer acceptable sacrifices. While his brother Huwai's offering was not accepted as worship, sacrifices and offerings are a matter of the state of the heart. The heart, which was the main part to be offered, was brought back to the house and Wapon knew straight away that a proper and acceptable sacrifice was not done.

As for his brother, Huwai took no notice of what nature had to offer him. It seems his heart was not straight. He was intent on destroying the blessings of his brother and brought destruction on both of them, just like Cain and Abel in the Bible. His life could have taken another direction if he took the time to notice God's beauty in creation and followed the footsteps of his brother, Wapon. God truly does reveal Himself in His creation and people just need to take the time in looking around to contemplate God in creation.

This section can be concluded by what the Psalmist has to say:

> *Praise the Lord, my soul! O Lord, my God, how great you are!*
>
> *You are clothed with majesty and glory; you cover yourself with light.*
>
> *You have spread out the heavens like a tent and built your home on the waters above.*
>
> *You use the clouds as your chariot and ride on the wings of the wind.*
>
> *You use the winds as your messengers and flashes of lightning as your servants.*
>
> *You have set the earth firmly on its foundations, and it will never be moved.*
>
> *You placed the ocean over it like a robe, and the water covered the mountains.*
>
> *When you rebuked the waters, they fled; they rushed away when they heard your shout of command.*
>
> *They flowed over the mountains and into the valleys, to the place you had made for them.*
>
> *You set a boundary they can never pass, to keep them from covering the earth again.*

You make springs flow in the valleys, and rivers run between the hills.

They provide water for the wild animals; there the wild donkeys quench their thirst.

In the trees near by, the birds make their nests and sing.

From the sky you send rain on the hills, and the earth is filled with your blessings.

You make grass grow for the cattle and plants for us to use, so that we can grow our crops and produce wine to make us happy, olive oil to make us cheerful, and bread to give us strength.

The cedars of Lebanon get plenty of rain - the L<small>ORD</small>'s own trees which He planted.

There the birds build their nests; the storks nest in the fir trees.

The wild goats live in the high mountains, and the rock badgers hide in the cliffs.

You created the moon to marked the months; the sun knows the time to set.

You made the night, and in the darkness all the wild animals comes out.

The young lions roar while they hunt, looking for the food that God provides.

When the sun rises, they go back and lie down in their dens.

Then people go out to do their work and keep working until evening.

L<small>ORD</small>, you have made so many things! How wisely you made them all!

The earth is filled with your creatures.

Psalm 104:1-24 [GNT]

When one thinks of the oceans so large and wide and all the countless creatures (small and large alike) that live in it, mountains, hills, valleys, rivers, deserts, trees, sky, moon, stars and all that is seen and unseen, we can only stand in awe of God's majesty. And to think that this almighty God took the time to reveal Himself in the culture and legends of the Mendi people. It's amazingly humbling to know His plan of Salvation for all mankind, regardless of skin colour, race, riches, classes, order etc. God is still in control and His ways are not our ways.

Footprint Eight

THE SECRET GROOM

This Legend contains several truths concerning how God planted His word in the legend culture of the people of Mendi Valley. Secret groom reveals the power of choice, the Holy Spirit Our Helper, and Jesus Christ our bride groom.

1. The Power of Choice

One gift that God gave humankind is the power to make decisions, or the gift of choice. When God created the first two human beings (Eve and Adam), He gave them the power of choice. That means the two of them had the power to choose to eat of the forbidden fruit, or to obey God and not eat it at all.

God gives people the free choice and free will to live their lives the way they desire. The gift of freedom of choice is the greatest gift that God can give to humankind. However, people who want to obey Him must make choices within the overall blueprint of His will. For what you choose to do and how you choose to live today determines your tomorrow, for one will reap what one sows. God's word stands to judge us all. No one can make a fool of the living God.

The power of choice means deciding where you want to go in life. It means that your choice today determines your future. God had spoken through His word that we are free to choose between good and evil. We may choose liberty and eternal life, or eternity in hell. That power of where we want to be tomorrow is in our choices in life, the power to choose that the Creator gave us.

In the legend, the brother of the girl goes on a long journey. The sister waited in anticipation. He chooses to bring an arrogant creature for a wife. This in turn brings separation and destruction to the family.

Seeing the choice her brother made, the young woman also needed to make her choice. For it was her responsibility to choose between a dead end like her brother or rewarding eternity as a member of God's family. She had to make her choice regarding her ultimate destiny. Choice was hers and hers alone to enable her to move on in her life. She had different possibilities, and she chose to climb the Palm tree with the little rat. She had chosen liberty and eternal life in the sky while her brother chose captivity and an unpleasant life on earth. It was the result of their choice between good and evil. They had made their bed and had to lie on it.

God created and gave mankind the gift of free will or the gift of choice. God is so powerful He could easily have us made like robots, programmed to do His every bidding. However, He didn't, as He made us for the purpose of relationship and love. Both of these are impossible where individuals have no power to choose.

Deuteronomy 30:19 [NLT] says:

> "Today I have given you the choice between life and death, between blessings and curses. Now I call on heaven and earth to witness the choice you make. Oh, that you would choose life..."

God is saying in His word that He is giving two choices. One is a path to life and another to death. One choice may release light and bring blessings, while the other one may fill with darkness, resulting in curses. For the path leads to two ways, one life and the other death, depending on which of two masters you serve (Christ or satan).

In the legend of the secret groom, both brother and sister had their own power to choose who to marry. The boy chooses to bring home a woman described more like a wicked witch. His choices are not made in righteousness, and now lead to pain, destruction and separation of his family. His choice brings with him demonic powers and works of the spirits of darkness, bringing pain, devastation, suffering, hurtful and lasting consequences.

As for the young girl, her choices are righteous and good and lead to a path of life, resulting in blessings and a good future. Her choices are indeed pleasing and leading to a right destiny. These were the results they had to live with for eternity, a direct result of their own choices. The power of choice is wonderfully embedded in this legend as God self-reveals Himself through this pagan culture.

2. *The Holy Spirit Our Helper*

The Holy Spirit, who is equal with God the Father and God the Son, is our helper, for the Bible says in Acts 1:4-5: [GNT]

> And when they came together, he [Jesus] gave them this order: "Do not leave Jerusalem, but wait for the gift I told you about, the gift my father promised. John baptised with water, but in a few days you will be baptised with the Holy Spirit'.

Jesus also says in John 14:16-17 [GNT]:

> I will ask the Father, and he will give you another Helper, who will stay with you forever. He is the Spirit, who reveals the truth about God.

The Holy Spirit teaches, guides, comforts and intercedes on our behalf every day. The Holy Spirit also plays a major role in the application of salvation to every human on earth. It is the Holy Spirit who brings conviction to the unbeliever and causes him to see the gospel in the clear light.

Another work of the Holy Spirit is to unite the believer with Christ enabling them to live a victorious life. The Holy Spirit also seals the believer, guaranteeing his or her security until the day of redemption.

In the Legend of the Secret Groom, the function of the Holy Spirit is seen. The young girl regretted not going with her boyfriend and found herself in a helpless situation. She was so depressed and in tears. She was also late and he had left - his dwelling area was empty; there was no one to be seen. All those who were living with him had taken off as well.

As she sat there crying in distress and desperation, a little rat appeared. The rat claimed to have been sent back by her boyfriend. Her boyfriend had gone up into the clouds in the sky. From high above the sky, he had seen her distress and sadness. He was here to help her and she had to get his advice if she wanted to go and be with the man and be happy again. The young girl was further convinced further when she was directed to a tall palm tree near her. She didn't know that a tree of this kind was nearby.

Onward and upward the rat led the young woman as she hang onto his tiny tail, for all her life dependent on this little animal. After all, he was the only one who seemed to know the way home to her boyfriend in the sky. They climbed until the rat safely delivered the girl into the waiting arms of her boyfriend.

The Holy Spirit is the only one who came down from heaven, sent by God the Father and Jesus the Son after His resurrection. After all works on earth are completed, only the Holy Spirit will lead us onward and upward to Heaven, for He is the one who teaches us the way to Heaven in Christ. The Holy Spirit will be the only one who will safely lead us onward and upward until He safely delivers us to our Heavenly Groom.

God in his powerful ways has set the person of the Holy Spirit within this beautiful legend that was told over and over again by our tribal elders.

Through his communications within our cultures, God has chosen to make Himself known to all human races including the people of Mendi Valley. God has also given us something invaluable that transcends culture, that is the Holy Spirit (John 16:13), who is a member of the trinity, sent to help reveal the truth.

3. Jesus Our Bridegroom

The bride is the body of true and faithful believers from both the Jewish and Gentile nations. This group of people have placed their complete trust and hope in the works of Jesus Christ as the promised Saviour. The bride of course is to be distinguished because she has a special and personal relationship with Jesus the groom.

The bridegroom's lifetime mission was to invite all mankind to trust in Jesus and become part of his bride (the church). Revelation 19:7-8 [GNT]:

> Let us rejoice and be glad; let us praise His greatness! For the time has come for the wedding of the Lamb, and His bride has prepared herself for it. She has been given clean shining linen to wear.

The bridegroom imagery of the Bible is a wonderful picture of the security of the children of God through their faith in Jesus Christ. Our security is unmoveable, as Psalms 91 says, whoever goes to the Lord for Protection, will find total security and safety in Him.

Picturing the church as a bride should keep our expectation alive regarding the return of the Lord Jesus as the Bridegroom. We the believers are the bride and our bridegroom is soon to return; what should bring greater joy to us than His glorious return. Revelation 21:1-2 [GNT]:

> Then I saw a new heaven and a new earth. The first heaven and the first earth disappeared, and the sea vanished. And I saw the Holy City, the new Jerusalem, coming down out of heaven from God, prepared and ready, like a bride dressed to meet her husband.

Heaven is the eternal and beautiful place where God draws near to us. This is the place where we will forever be in intimate fellowship with Him. Knowing that Christ loves us and wants us to live with Him forever is quite exciting and should be something that every bride should be looking forward to.

Being part of the bride of the Lord Jesus Christ is a privilege, for privileged are those who receive salvation. For the Word of God will completely beautify and perfect them, getting ready for the wedding day with Him.

On the wedding day, all of heaven will be captivated as the most beautiful bride walks down the aisle of Heaven. Jesus will be waiting and I believe He will be the most attractive being in the whole cosmos. The bride will be overjoyed to see Him and He will also be overjoyed to see His bride, for He had sacrificed Himself for His bride. To Jesus, the Church is His glorious, beautiful and perfect bride. Millions and millions of believers across the world are part of this glorious day.

The young girl in the legend trusted that she will somehow find her safety in her boyfriend. Because of her trust, she followed the leading of the rat who represented the Holy Spirit, and the gates of hell never overcame her. After being delivered safely into the arms of the bridegroom, having left earth below, she finds herself in a bigger wedding party in the sky.

It's her golden privilege to be in the groom's wedding party, for she finds out she is not the only one. There were so many others also there for the wedding. She had received the offer and had accepted it. She now finds herself in a new place where a great wedding is going on. She definitely was part of something huge. In the legend she is said to be living happily ever after.

As for her brother, he had made a wrong choice, in disobedience or against his inner voice of the Holy Spirit. His choice resulted in the release of demonic powers within the spirits of spiritual darkness, resulting in lasting evil consequences on earth.

For every choice has consequences, some good and some bad. His decision affected his whole future. He had chosen satan as his master, while the girl chose life and light in Jesus Christ. She ends up in the sky and became part of a bigger wedding party. It truly was a happy ending for her.

Our God is an awesome God to embed something so important from His word in this legend of the folk of Mendi valley in a faraway land. God surely is an omnipotent God. He was present among these pagan people and chose to plant this message in their very own culture.

As a result, the people of the valley received the gospel easily, as it was not so foreign to their cultural legends.

Footprint Nine

WAR WITH THE GIANTS

This legend was the story of the existence of Nephillim or Giants on Earth. Giants existed and were at war with the Israelites. For instance, the Israelites at war with the Philistine Giants, like the famous story of David and Goliath, or the total destruction of giants by Joshua.

Nephillim or Giants, who are referenced in the books of Genesis and Numbers, were a group of mysterious beings of larger size and strength, who lived both before Noah and after the flood. Giants are taken to mean the fallen angels, because of the Hebrew word 'Nephal' which means to fall.

The Nephillim are mentioned just before the flood in Genesis 6:4 [NASB].

> The Nephillim were on the earth in those days, and also afterward, when the sons of God came in to the daughters of men, and they bore children to them. Those were the mighty men who were of old, men of renown.

It is further stated that as the Israelites prepared to enter Canaan, the Promised Land, after their long journey from Egypt, they also saw giants. Numbers 13:33 [ESV] states:

> And there we saw the Nephillim (sons of Anak who come from the Nephilim), and we seemed to ourselves like grasshoppers..

The Scriptures here indicates they were bigger in size and strength than normal humans.

Considering the purpose of the creation of the earth, the Scriptures make it clear it was to provide a place for the sons and daughters of God to dwell in morality, through keeping His word and returning to the presence of God. After God created mankind (male and female) in His own image,

> God blessed them; and God said to them, "Be fruitful and multiply, and fill the earth, and subdue it."
>
> Genesis 2:24 [NASB]

God's ultimate plan for humanity was to enjoy the beauty, abundance, fruitfulness and growth of His creation. The Garden of Eden was set in an idyllic manner, as humankind was intended to prosper in every sense. In the garden God provided an abundance of resources and means for humans to flourish. Multiplication, expansion, stewardship and dominion are part of God's divine plan. Genesis chapter 1 and 2 teach us about those things.

However, just like the disobedience in the Garden of Eden by the first humans (Eve and Adam), there was also disobedience in Heaven which saw the downfall of Lucifer and his followers. The fallen angels then slept with human women, producing giants who terrorised the people of the earth due to their large bodies and much bigger size and strength.

It is evident over and over again, especially in the Old Testament, that terrifying giants did live. Deuteronomy 3:11 for instance describes the giant's coffin as made of stones, four metres long and two metres wide. It is also stated in 1 Samuel 17:4 that the famous Goliath from the armies of the Philistines, who was defeated by young David, was a giant.

2 Samuel 21:20 also talks about a war taking place at Gath where there was a man of great stature who had six fingers

on his hand and six toes, and had been born to the giants. Furthermore, the Bible describes the Israelites contact and description of the giants:

> Where can we go up? Our brethren have made our hearts melt, saying, "The people are bigger and taller than we; the cities are large and fortified to heaven. And besides; we saw the sons of Anakim there.
>
> Deuteronomy 1:28 [NASB]

> ... a people great and tall, the sons of Anakim, whom you know and whom you have heard it said, 'Who can stand before the sons of Anak?'
>
> Dueteronomy 9:2 [NASB]

Despite their terrifying size and strength, God had great plans to destroy such people using great men like David and Joshua. 1 Samuel 17:41-54 for instance, tells the story of David, who uses a small stone to kill the Giant Goliath, who defiles the name of the God of Israel. David won the victory in the name of God almighty.

> And David put his hand into his bag and took from it a stone and slung it, and struck the Philistine on his forehead. And the stone sank into his forehead. And the stone sank into his forehead so that he fell on his face to the ground.
>
> Thus David prevailed over the Philistine with a sling and a stone and he stuck the Philistine and killed him, but there was no sword in David's hand.
>
> 1 Samuel 17: 49-50 [NASB]

Joshua is another example, who managed to totally destroy the giant's cities which stood in his way as the children of Israel advanced to settle in their promised land. Joshua 11:21 [NASB]:

> Then Joshua came at that time and cut off the Anakim from ... all the hill country of Judah and from the hill country of Israel. Josuha utterly destroyed them with their cities.

God was behind all this defeat of the giants. Amos the Prophet states in Amos 2:9 [NASB]:

Yet it was I who destroyed the Amorite before them,

Though his height was like the height of cedars

And he was as strong as oaks;

I even destroyed his fruit above and his root below.

The Legend is that Tella Hin and Tuk Ten Piu, despite their sizes, were able to wipe out the giants, that is, their fruit above and roots below, just like what Prophet Amos is prophesying in Amos 2:9. Coincidence eh? No, it's not coincidence but God working wonders in our own unique cultures. God gives prior witness of His existence to make way for the gospel of Jesus which was going to be preached to the furthest corner of the world.

This great and almighty God, our defender, refuge and strength, who is always ready to help in times of trouble, decided to plant the story of the giants and how they can be defeated, in the Legend of the War with the Giants of the children of Mendi Valley.

Footprint Ten

THE CALL OF THE RISING SMOKE IN THE BLUE MOUNTAIN

This legend tells of the call for daily sacrifices by the Israelites for various reasons. This was hinted at by the smoke that rose forever. It also draws light on the different parts of the Tabernacle or Temple of God, where sacrifices were taking place. This legend is purely about the division of the Temple of God and the daily sacrifices that the Israelites were offering.

Specific discussions will be on exposing the hidden truths in the legend on Sacrifices and Offerings, and Division of the Tabernacle or Temple (Court Yard, Holy Place and the Holy of Holies).

I. Sacrifices and Offerings

Sacrifices are something that is brought before the altar as a sacrificial present, costing a sacrifical life, while an offering is a gift brought before God with humility and due honour. An offering doesn't have to be an animal but giving to the Lord whatever He requires. This could be our time, our earthly processions or our energies to further His works.

The Old Testament scriptures talk a lot about sacrifices and offerings. Sacrifices and offerings started with Cain and Abel and continued for a long time until the destruction of the temple in Jerusalem in 70AD. The main offerings commanded by God are the Burnt offerings, the Meal offering, the Peace offering, the Sin offering, the Trespass offering and the Drink offering.

Of all those offerings, it seems that, in the Legend of 'the calling of the smoke that goes on forever', one is reminded of the continual Burnt offering. This kind of offering, which is also known as an ascending offering, is where offerings are wholly burnt at the altar and the smoke rises forever, and is first seen even before the times of Moses. Noah offered burnt offerings as indicated in Genesis 8:20, as did Abraham in Genesis 22:2, then the times of Job (Job1:5) all the way through to Moses.

In this kind of offering, one lamb was to be offered every morning and evening (Exodus 29:42) at the temple. The fire would burn throughout the day. Also, according to Numbers 28:9-10, on top of the continual burning, two lambs were offered on the Sabbath, so the smoke rose forever, even on the day of rest a fire was built and a burnt offering was done.

At the beginning of the month, Burnt offerings were also happening (Numbers 28:11), when two young bullocks, one ram and seven lambs were offered. Burnt offerings also happened at the seven feasts at the time of the Passover festival (2 Chronicles 30:24, Numbers 28:24). This offering also took place for the consecration of Priests (Leviticus 8:18), of people (Leviticus 9:3-7) and of Levites (Number 8:12).

Burnt offerings were further done for the dedication of altars (Numbers 7:87) and temples (1 Kings 8:64). They were also made for cleansing of women bearing children (Leviticus 12:6), lepers (Leviticus 14:19) and cleansing of people with some kind of bodily discharge (Leviticus 15:15).

Every single day or month, every feast in consecration, dedication, cleansing and completion of Oaths and burnt offering was a direct command from God, reminding the children of Israel again and again that God Yahweh was the Holy One, and He alone was God who took pleasure in such offerings.

Finally there was also the freewill Burnt offering where individuals brought voluntary offerings as per the instruction in Leviticus 22:18. In some offerings, the offerer and the priest shared in eating a part of it, but in the burnt offering they burnt it whole to God. When the animal was burnt wholly on the altar it gave a pleasant smell to God (Leviticus 1:9). As long as the Israelites existed, a burnt offering needed to be done, thus the fire for the burnt offering was continually alight.

While all these sacrifices were going on with the Israelites on a daily basis, the legend about the rising smoke, that went on forever and had the power to pull the mother and daughter, was told over and over in a totally different environment, in Papua New Guinea in the Mendi Valley. God is bringing the systems of burnt offerings and sacrifices to this group of people in the story of their legend.

God's grace had been at work in the cultures of the children of Mendi Valley, preparing the hearts of a faraway pagan people to receive the Gospel and true light that only the Gospel can bring. Thankfully, we can see the gospel of truth also working within our cultures, only because God had planted eternity in their hearts by leaving His footprint in their cultures.

The Lord of the whole universe cares enough to plant such an important part of the holy living cultures of His chosen people into cultures that belonged to Gentiles and lost tribal nations. His love is undeserving and endures forever. It's baffling and humbling yet glorious and powerful to know His eternal love that endures forever for people great and small, rich and poor, holy and pagan, old and young people of the whole world. His salvation plan works for people from all corners of the world because the Lord of the Universe loves all the people of the world. That's why He gave His son, so that "whoever believes in Him may not perish but have eternal Life" (John 3:16).

2. Division of the Tabernacle or Temple

As the children of Israel left Egypt and journeyed through the wilderness, God commanded Moses their leader to build a Tabernacle, so that He would dwell on earth among His chosen people at that time. From the fall of Eve and Adam in Genesis until the construction of the Tabernacle, the Bible records people occasionally talking and walking with God, but not God dwelling with them. While the Children of Israel wandered in the wilderness, the tabernacle was the dwelling place of God and He journeyed with them wherever they went. After entering Canaan, the Promised Land, where they settled, they built a permanent tabernacle of stone, known as the Holy Temple. The contents of the temple were similar to the tabernacle having three parts (outer court, Holy place and Holy of Holies).

On Mt. Sinai, Moses not only received the Ten Commandments but also the detailed instructions for building a meeting place for God and His people. It is within the framework of this Old Testament sanctuary that God draws His people closer to Himself through a detailed sacrificial sytem. This was purposely set to provide a possible means for God's people to dwell with Him (Exodus 25:8).

The tabernacle was divided into three parts (outer court, holy place and Holy of Holies).

a. Outer Court

The outside area of the tabernacle was known as the outer court. In ancient times as recorded in the Old Testament, this was where the children of Israel came to worship God. At the entrance of the tabernacle, in the outer court, was the alter for burnt offerings, where common people offered sacrifices to God. The outer court was a common place where everyone who is called to make an offering and sacrifices comes in. In the outer court, only the altar for offering your sacrifice and the laver for washing yourself were found.

In the legend, the place where the two ladies go every day to look for a way to the top of the rock, where they could see the man who appears on the hill above the waterfall, represents the outer courtyard.

b. Holy Place

The internal tabernacle was divided into the Holy Place and the Holy of Holies. A small number of priests entered the Holy Place where the showbread table, the light and the incense to please God were. In the Holy Place there is a light that goes on forever, a showbread table and the incense to please God.

In the legend, the two ladies entering the area on top of the hill, where nobody had ever entered before, represented the Holy Place. That place was much better than the outer yard just like the Holy Place was much better than the outer court. The man they saw from below was not there, but his most recent activities showed His presence close by. Further investigation leads them to the Lake. In here only one has to enter with a rope tied to their leg. This leads to the High Priest and His activities beyond the thick curtain which the lake represents.

c. Holy of Holies

This was the holiest place and so only the High Priest would enter once a year. To enter the Holy of Holies the High Priest had to pass through the gate of the outer court first. Then they pass into the Holy Place, then the Holiest place last.

In the Holy of Holies was the 'Ark of the Covenant', a box overlaid with gold. Found within the ark was a golden urn holding manna and Aron's staff that budded, and the tablets of the covenant. The ark had a cover made of pure gold. This cover was the Throne of Grace. When the priest entered this place, he would immediately sprinkle blood on this cover. When God came down, His Glory rested above the mercy seat between the cherubim facing each other. It was on this cover that God forgave the sins of the people and it was also here that God fellowshipped and spoke with the High Priest. It was the Throne of Grace, the place for God to show unmerited favour to man.

In the legend, the lake represents the thick curtain that separates the Holy place from the Holy of Holies. This is because the girl entered the lake and immediately found herself on the other side of the world. She was not even wet. She finds the young man, who is represented in this legend as Jesus Christ, being the High Priest. She had entered the place where the Throne of Grace stands. Because this was the place that God gave grace to mankind, she found grace and favour from this stranger.

As for the two ladies in the legend, they have experienced the altar of burnt offering, signifying the Cross, and the laver representing the cleansing power of the Holy Spirit, in the outer court. Only after that experience were they able to enter the Holy place.

Upon entering the top of the rock, they were able to feast on the food left behind by the man they saw on top of the hill. This signifies the fact that, entering the holy place, they are enjoying Christ here as the showbread and the bread of life. At this point, the two ladies are experiencing Christ more. However, one has to enter the Holy of Holiest to fully enjoy Christ Himself. That's when the young girl pressed on and entered the Holy of Holies and enjoys Him at the ark in the Holy of Holies.

By embedding this very important part of the daily worship of God in this Legend, God preserves a key truth in the most strangest of cultures. He does this to prepare the hearts of this group of people to accept and acknowledge the one true God when the time is right. And when God sent his missionaries, that is when the time was right and the people of the valley gladly received the Gospel without putting up much resistance. After all, their own teachings were very similar to those that the missionaries brought.

To conclude this chapter, one can see that God has prepared this group of people to receive the message of Jesus Christ by giving prior witness of His existence through their every day to day culture. If God gave prior witness to Himself in other cultures around the world, would He not do the same thing for this people? For the pagan people in this part of the land seemed to be prepared for the Gospel as they readily received it without putting up much resistence. This happened because the message they were receiving was nothing new, as they had been hearing this in their day to day cultural legends. God's ultimate purpose was that, from Eden, His presence should be extended to the ends of the earth.

God is truly the Alpha and the Omega.....

www.ingramcontent.com/pod-product-compliance
Lightning Source LLC
Chambersburg PA
CBHW072336300426
44109CB00042B/1636